BY SARAH MAXWELL AND DOLORES SMITH

Women OF Influence

12 LEADERS OF THE SUFFRAGE MOVEMENT

A Block-of-the-Month Quilt

KANSAS CITY STAR QUILTS

Continuing the Tradition

Women of Influence
12 Leaders of the Suffrage Movement
A Block-of-the-Month Quilt
BY SARAH MAXWELL AND DOLORES SMITH

Editor: Jenifer Dick
Designer: Amy Robertson
Photography: Aaron T. Leimkuehler
Portrait Paintings: Brian Grubb
Illustration: Eric Sears
Technical Editor: Jane Miller
Production Assistance: Jo Ann Groves

Published by:
Kansas City Star Books
1729 Grand Blvd.
Kansas City, Missouri, USA 64108

First edition, first printing
ISBN: 978-1-935362-18-0

Library of Congress Control Number: 2009932584

Printed in the United States of America
by Walsworth Publishing Co., Marceline, MO

To order copies, call StarInfo at (816) 234-4636 and say "Books."

The Quilter's Home Page

THIS BOOK IS DEDICATED
To these 12 women and all the others who selflessly work to better the world for everyone.

SARAH MAXWELL

To the women who played a major part in the women's movement. Not only did they work to give women the right to vote, but they opened the doors to give women a voice in the world and a right to dream and follow their dreams. These woman made it possible for women today to achieve what each one of us is capable of doing and more.

DOLORES SMITH

Contents

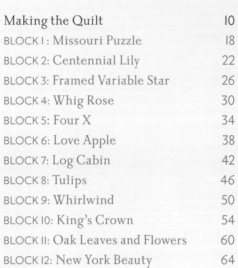

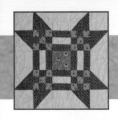

About the Authors

Dolores Smith, left, and Sarah Maxwell

Dolores Smith and Sarah Maxwell opened Homestead Hearth in September 2002. For many years prior to that, they traveled to quilt shows around the country and visited shops along the way. Always, they talked about having their own shop and all of the exciting things they would do if they owned a shop. The reality of owning the shop and its related experiences has far exceeded their dreams.

Under the trade name of Homestead Hearth, Dolores and Sarah have designed quilts for use at the International Quilt Market and have created patterns for fabric company websites. They are regular contributors to McCall's Quilting and Quick Quilts magazines. Their work has also appeared in most of the other major quilting magazines.

They debuted their own pattern line in May 2009 and will sell an extensive line of original patterns starting this October. You can find their patterns and many other items at their website, www.homestead-hearth.com.

Dolores lives in Mexico, Mo., with her husband. She has two sons. Sarah also lives in Mexico with her husband. She has two daughters. This is their first book.

Writing a book is a project that involves many people in addition to the authors. As we worked through this, our first book, we learned that a whole team of people are responsible for bringing any book into print.

Creating a book is a very technical process and we could not have completed the task without the expert staff at the *Kansas City Star Books*. Thanks to Doug Weaver and Diane McLendon for selecting our design for the 2009 block of the month project. Thanks to Jenifer Dick for her expertise in editing – her knowledge and suggestions undoubtedly made this a better final product. Thanks to Aaron Leimkuehler for the gorgeous photographs of our quilts. Until you actually do it, no one would believe that photographing an inanimate object could take so much preparation and time. Aaron made it look easy and made our quilts look fantastic. Thanks to Amy Robertson for the beautiful design of this book. And thanks to Eric Sears for the artwork illustrating our patterns and Jane Miller for the technical editing of our patterns.

When we first thought about submitting a design for the 2009 block of the month, we wanted to create something that really helped shop owners offer their customers a way to recreate our sample quilts as we originally made them. Marcus Fabrics was invaluable in making this happen. From working with us to put together a fabric line for the quilts to keeping the fabrics in print for the duration of the program, the staff at Marcus has set a new standard for excellence in working with shop owners and customers. We send a special thanks to Pati Violick, Indra Rampersaud and Stephanie Dell'Olio at Marcus for their support and contributions to this project.

Finally, thanks to the Audrain County Historical Society for allowing us to photograph at their facility. The museum is one of the gems of mid-Missouri and we are so happy that we can share some of the unique collections in these photographs. *—Sarah and Dolores*

Sarah writes: As deadlines loom, the author's family often discovers that they are drawn into the process for advice, encouragement and assistance. "Thank you" really doesn't adequately convey my gratitude to my family for all of their support during all of the work to make the quilts, write the patterns and write the text for this book. My husband, Joe, always offers his proofreading and analytical skills and tolerates my lack of domesticity while I work on these projects. Daughters Megan and Shannen are ready to offer advice on quilting designs and color and listen to me talk about ran-

dom bits of trivia I've discovered in my research. My parents, Virgil Baker and Jo Turchie, provide encouragement and support and always remind me not to work too much. My mother-in-law, Molly Maxwell Shellabarger helped coordinate the location for the photography in this book and makes sure my family gets fed when I'm working late. So, thanks to all of my family for supporting me through this adventure of writing a book. Thanks to Dolores Smith for dreaming about a quilt store with me for so many years and then diving into all the challenges of owning a business. Dolores never says no when I spring my latest idea on her and I appreciate her consistent willingness to keep trying new things.*—SM*

Dolores writes: To my husband, Brian, of 27 years—there is no one else I can imagine sharing my life with. Thank you for all your sacrifices and being there to allow all my dreams to come true.

Ryan and Breigha, my oldest son and his soul mate—even though they are no longer with us, their smiling faces will be with me every day. Thank you for all your help in getting our doors open and for being both families' guardian angels.

Kyle, my youngest son, thank you for your honesty and playful spirit and helping me and your dad through the roughest time in our lives. May you be blessed in the future with wonderful children as your dad and I have been. But, most of all I want to thank you—you and your brother—for picking me to be your mother. I could always count on you to give me your honest opinion when working on a quilt whether it be on color or the design. Always follow your dreams.

And then, there is my extended family, or just putting it simply, my family. Sarah, thank you for being a good friend and for picking me to be a part of this adventure. Dawn, just plain thank you for being there and your help in making sure I met my deadlines. And, last but not least all the women who work in the shop, Lori, Jane, Brooke, Megan and Sue —and my mom, Gladys, who has moved, but was there in the beginning. They are not employees, but family.

Connie thank you for all the awesome quilting and meeting me at McDonald's day or night to get that quilt on the frame to make the deadlines. And to the Historical Society for giving us a beautiful place to take pictures.

And for all of our customers that have made this possible. *—DS*

Women of Influence

THE LONG FIGHT FOR WOMEN'S SUFFRAGE

While many Americans can name Susan B. Anthony as a leader in the fight for voting rights for women, few recall that many other citizens were active in the decades-long fight for suffrage. Several of these women sacrificed their personal lives to fight on behalf of others. This book highlights 12 of those women.

Throughout much of America's fledgling growth as a country, men voted in elections and women stayed home without questioning the situation. However, by the mid-1800s, a growing group of women who were questioning things like alcohol use and slavery also began to question why the men of the country were allowed to make all major decisions about the direction of the country. Several of the leaders were Quakers, a religious denomination that generally promoted equality between the sexes. As these women who were used to some measure of equality at home and within their own communities encountered discrimination in public domains, their sense that change was needed grew.

Lucretia Mott and Elizabeth Cady Stanton were two such women. They met when both were refused seats at the World Anti-Slavery Convention in London. Over the next few years, Mott and Stanton kept in touch and discussed their concerns about the treatment of women in American society on issues such as fair wages, property and divorce laws and education. They became convinced that the only way to fix these problems was by gaining a voice in the political process. As a result, the Seneca Falls Convention was convened in 1848 to formally address women's equality. Stanton drafted the document which was the official policy statement for the convention, the "Declaration of Sentiments." In concluding the document, she argued that women must secure the right to vote. Some in her circle of friends, including Mott were shocked by this idea but Stanton insisted on including the request saying "I saw clearly that the power to make the laws was the right through which all other rights could be secured."

The struggle for the right to vote became entwined with the issue of slavery especially during the Civil War years. Women like Susan Anthony and Lucy Stone were active in both the abolitionist movement to end slavery along with the suffrage movement. When the Civil War ended, the suffrage movement

> "I think that the young women of today do not and can never know at what price their right to free speech and to speak at all in public has been earned."
>
> LUCY STONE

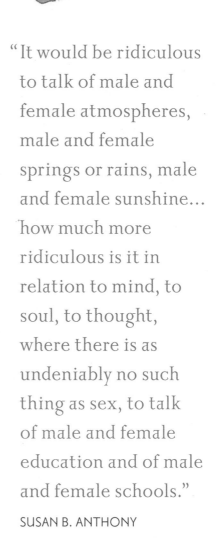

splintered as one group supported the Fifteenth Amendment which granted black men the right to vote while a second group argued that women should be included in the Fifteenth Amendment. The first group believed that change would be more likely to occur in incremental steps so granting another group of men the vote would naturally lead to granting women the vote at some point in the future. In contrast, the second group argued that there was no point to changing the Constitution unless the change helped everyone.

For a while, this split slowed the progress of the suffrage movement. As the United States fought in World War I, however, a leader emerged who understood some of the political dynamics necessary to secure passage of an issue that divided so many people. Carrie Catt was willing to forego some of the earlier rhetoric which had slowed progress on the issue and instead sought compromise with members of Congress, state legislatures and President Woodrow Wilson. Ultimately her efforts were successful and when Tennessee ratified the Nineteenth Amendment in 1920, it became the required 36th state to approve the language thereby making the women's right to vote a reality.

Despite passage of the Nineteenth Amendment, not everyone was ready to support suffrage. The remaining 12 states (of the original 48) took more than 60 years to pass the amendment. Not until 1984, did the last of these 48 states, Mississippi, actually approve the amendment.

This book tells the story of 12 women who influenced the direction of the United States and secured a fundamental right for more than half of its citizens—the right to vote.

THE 19TH AMENDMENT:

Section 1. The right of the citizens of the United States to vote shall not be denied or abridged by the United States or by any State on account of sex.

"It would be ridiculous to talk of male and female atmospheres, male and female springs or rains, male and female sunshine… how much more ridiculous is it in relation to mind, to soul, to thought, where there is as undeniably no such thing as sex, to talk of male and female education and of male and female schools."

SUSAN B. ANTHONY

Sisters in Suffrage
Made by Sarah Maxwell • Quilted by Connie Gresham

Making the Quilt

Women of Influence is a 12–block sampler quilt set with a Framing Star around each block. A pieced inner border and a plain outer border finish the quilt.

Instructions to make the 12 blocks that comprise the quilt are found on the following pages. Make one of each of the blocks. Once the blocks are done, make the Framing Star block to surround each block. Then add the borders to finish the quilt.

To Make the Framing Star
The templates for the Framing Star and the inner border are found on page xx.

Note: If you wish to recreate Sarah's quilt using the same fabrics she used, see Reproducing Sisters in Suffrage on page 16.

To construct this Framing Star block, cut as follows:

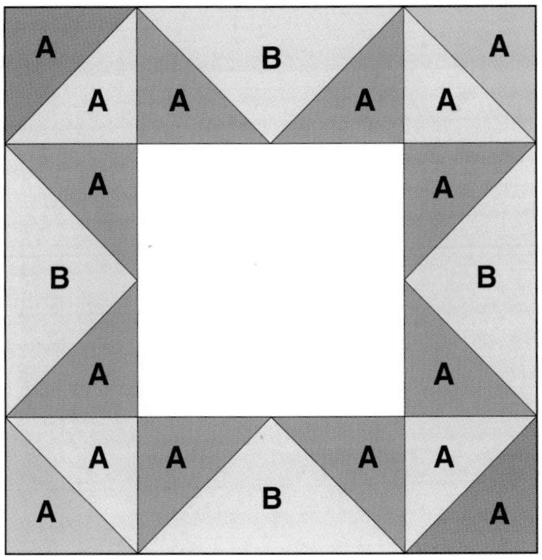

From tan floral cut:
* 4 – A triangles. Cut 2 – 6⅞" x 6⅞" squares. Cut the squares from corner to corner once on the diagonal or use template A.
* 4 – B triangles. Cut 1 – 13¼" x 13¼" square. Cut the square from corner to corner on both diagonals or use template B.

Fabrics required to make 12 blocks
Block Backgrounds – 1 ¾ yard
Assorted Greens – ⅞ yard
Assorted Pinks & Reds – 1 yard
Assorted Browns & Golds – 1 yard
Assorted Blacks – ⅝ yard
Assorted Blues – ½ yard

Fabrics for the Framing Stars, borders and binding
Red Floral: 1 yard
Tan Floral: 4 yards
Blue Print: 2 yards
Tan Print: 1 yard
Blue Floral: 3 yards

From the tan print cut:

✳ 2 – A triangles. Cut 1 – 6⅞" x 6⅞" square. Cut the square from corner to corner once on the diagonal or use template A.

From the red floral cut:

✳ 2 – A triangles. Cut 1 – 6⅞" x 6⅞" square. Cut the squares from corner to corner once on the diagonal or use template A.

From the blue print cut:

✳ 8 – A triangles. Cut 4 – 6⅞" x 6⅞" squares. Cut the squares from corner to corner once on the diagonal or use template A.

Piecing Directions

✳ Sew 1 blue triangle A to each short edge of 1 background triangle B to make a rectangle unit. Repeat to make four units.

✳ Sew 2 rectangle units to opposite sides of a finished block.

✳ Sew 1 red triangle A to 1 background triangle A to make a half–square triangle unit. Repeat to make 2 red/background half–square triangle units.

✳ Sew 1 light brown triangle A to 1 background triangle A to make a half–square triangle unit. Repeat to make 2 light brown/background half–square triangle units.

✳ Sew these half–square triangle units to opposite ends of the remaining 2 rectangles referring to the color diagram for proper placement.

✳ Sew these units together to form the framed block.

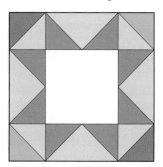

Quilt top assembly

✳ Once the Framing Star points are sewn on all 12 bocks, lay them out in 4 rows of 3 blocks to match the quilt assembly diagram. Sew blocks together. Join the rows.

Borders

Inner pieced border

From tan floral cut:

✳ 28 – A triangles. Cut 14 – 6⅞" x 6⅞" squares. Cut the squares from corner to corner once on the diagonal or use template A.

From the tan print cut:

✳ 16 – A triangles. Cut 8 – 6⅞" x 6⅞" square. Cut the square from corner to corner once on the diagonal or use template A.

From the red floral cut:

✳ 16 – A triangles. Cut 8 – 6⅞" x 6⅞" square. Cut the squares from corner to corner once on the diagonal or use template A.

From the blue floral cut:

✳ 60 – A triangles. Cut 30 – 6⅞" x 6⅞" squares. Cut the squares from corner to corner once on the diagonal or use template A.

✳ The pieced inner border is composed of 60 – 6½" unfinished half–square triangle units. To make the units, sew a blue floral A triangle to each of the red floral, tan print and tan floral A triangles.

Make 16

Make 16

Make 28

✳ Referring to the assembly diagram, arrange the half–square triangle units as shown. The 2 side borders consist of 16 half–square triangle units each. The top and bottom borders consist of 14 units each. Make sure the units are turned correctly to create the hour–glass and square shapes along the edge of the quilt. Sew each side border on first, then sew the top and bottom borders to the quilt top.

Outer border

✳ Measure the quilt top from top to bottom in the middle. From blue floral, cut strips from the width of fabric that are 4½" wide. Sew 2 rows and cut to the length of the quilt top. Sew to the sides of the top. Measure the quilt top again from side to side in the middle to get the length for the top and bottom borders. Sew 4½" strips to this measurement and stitch to the top and bottom of the quilt.

✳ Quilt as desired and bind with the blue floral.

The photos in "Women of Influence" were taken on location at Graceland Museum in Mexico, Missouri. Graceland was built in 1857 by John P. Clark. During the earliest part of the Civil War, the home was host to Col. Ulysses S. Grant. Today, visitors can view the home to see its Victorian elegance as well as the history of the county. For more information, visit www.audrain.org.

Women of Influence
Made by Dolores Smith • Quilted by Connie Gresham

Reproducing Sisters in Suffrage

Sarah used Marcus Fabrics to make her version of the Women of Influence quilt, Sisters in Suffrage. In support of this book, they have agreed to keep the fabric available until Spring 2010 so you can recreate Sarah's quilt exactly. Use the reference numbers below or visit www. homesteadhearth.com.

Fabrics required for the Framing Stars, border and binding:
* Red floral (R33 Sturbridge Village IV 1379–011): 1 yard
* Tan floral (R33 Sturbridge Village IV 1291–0140): 4 yards
* Blue print (R33 Sturbridge Village IV 1284–0150): 2 yards
* Tan Print (R22 Bonnie Blue Basics and Backgrounds 1041–0188): 1 yard
* Blue Floral (R33 Merrimack N559–197D): 3 yards

Fabrics required for the 12 blocks:
For the blocks, you will need a fat quarter or less of these Marcus Brothers fabrics.
* R22 Bonnie Blue Basics and Backgrounds: 1037–0188, 1039–0111, 1038–126, 1032–0111, 1034–0112, 1041–0128, 1037–0120, 1035–0126, 1034–0114, 1034–0111, 1039–0188, 1032–0120, 1033–0113
* R33 Vicksburg: N949–0150, N952–0113, N958–0150, N949–0113, N958–0113
* R33 Classic Sturbridge Village: N872–114, N879–114, N452–161D, N454–189D, N447–189D, N870–114D, N877–114D, N454–161D, N446–161D, N453–161D
* R33 Nineteenth Century Backgrounds II: N292–160, N295–160T, N291–160T, N299–160, N296–160
* R33 Sturbridge Village IV: 1290–0111, 1295–0111, 1290–0140, 1283–0140, 1289–140, 1284–0140, 1292–0111, 1379–0111
* R33 Inkwell: 1365–0194, 1366–0125, 1370–0112

Fabrics used for each block:

Block 1—Missouri Puzzle
* Background (R22 Bonnie Blue Basics and Backgrounds 1037–0188)
* Red Print (R22 Bonnie Blue Basics and Backgrounds 1039–0111)
* Blue Print (R33 Vicksburg 949–0150)
* Brown Print (R33 Vicksburg 952–0113)

Block 2—Centenniel Lily
* Background (R33 Nineteenth Century Backgrounds II N292–160T)
* Red Print (R22 Bonnie Blue Basics and Backgrounds 1032–0111)
* Pink Print (R22 Bonnie Blue Basics and Backgrounds 1038–0126)
* Green Print No. 1 (R33 Classic Sturbridge Village N879–0114D)
* Green Print No. 2 (R33 Classic Sturbridge Village N872–114D)

Block 3—Framed Variable Star
* Background 1 (R33 Inkwell 1366–0125)
* Background 2 (R22 Bonnie Blue Basics and Backgrounds 1037–0188)
* Red Print (R33 Sturbridge Village 1295–0111)
* Green Print (R22 Bonnie Blue Basics and Backgrounds 1034–0114)
* Black Print (R33 Inkwell 1370–0112)

Block 4—Whig Rose
* Background (R33 Classic Sturbridge Village N453–161D)
* Red Print (R33 Sturbridge Village IV 1295–0111)
* Pink Print (R22 Bonnie Blue Basics and Backgrounds 1038–0126)
* Blue Print: (R22 Bonnie Blue Basics and Backgrounds 1032–120)
* Brown Print: (R22 Bonnie Blue Basics and Backgrounds 1033–113)
* Green Print #1 (R33 Classic Sturbridge Village N870–114D)
* Green Print #2 (R33 Classic Sturbridge Village N877–114D)

Block 5—Four X
* Background Print (R33 Sturbridge Village IV 1283–0140)
* Brown Print (R33 Vicksburg N949–0113)
* Blue Print (R33 Vicksburg N958–0150)

Block 6—Love Apple
* Background (R33 Nineteenth Century Backgrounds II N299–160T)
* Red Print 1 (R33 Classic Sturbridge Village N446–161D)
* Red Print 2 (R33 Sturbridge Village IV 1379–0111)
* Red Print 3 (R22 Bonnie Blue Basics and Backgrounds 1034–0111)
* Green Print (R33 Classic Sturbridge Village N877–114D)
* Gold Print (R22 Bonnie Blue Basics and Backgrounds 1039–0188)

Block 7—Log Cabin
* Black (R22 Bonnie Blue Basics and Backgrounds 1034–112)
* Light Brown Print 1 (R33 Classic Sturbridge Village N447–189)
* Medium Brown Print 2 (R33 Sturbridge Village IV 1283–0140)
* Dark Brown Print 3 (R33 Sturbridge Village IV 1290–0140)
* Light Red Print 1 (R33 Sturbridge Village IV 1290–0111)
* Medium Red Print 2 (R33 Classic Sturbridge Village N452–161D)
* Dark Red Print 3 (R33 Sturbridge Village IV 1295–0111)

Block 8—Tulips
* Background (R33 Nineteenth Century Backgrounds II N296–160T)
* Red Print 1 (R33 Classic Sturbridge Village N454–161D)
* Red Print 2 (R33 Classic Sturbridge Village N446–161D)
* Green Print 1 (R33 Classic Sturbridge Village N877–114D)
* Green Print 2 (R33 Classic Sturbridge Village N870–114D)

Block 9—Whirlwind
* Background Print (R33 Sturbridge Village IV 1292–0111)
* Brown Print (R33 Sturbridge Village IV 1284–0140)

Block 10—King's Crown
* Background #1 Print (R33 Nineteenth Century Backgrounds II N291–160T)
* Background #2 Print (R33 Sturbridge Village IV 1292–0111)
* Gold Print (R33 Sturbridge Village IV 1289–0140)
* Red #1 Print (R33 Classic Sturbridge Village N446–161D)
* Red #2 Print (R33 Classic Sturbridge Village N452–161D)
* Brown #1 Print (R33 Vicksburg N958–0113)
* Brown #2 Print (R33 Vicksburg N949–0113)

Block 11—Oak Leaves and Flowers
* Background (R33 Inkwell 1365–194)
* Black Print (R22 Bonnie Blue Basics and Backgrounds 1034–0112)
* Red Print (R22 Bonnie Blue Basics and Backgrounds 1035–0126)
* Blue Print (R22 Bonnie Blue Basics and Backgrounds 1037–0120)
* Beige Print (R22 Bonnie Blue Basics and Backgrounds 1041–0128)

Block 12—New York Beauty
* Background Print (R33 Nineteenth Century II N296–160T)
* Light Red Print (R33 Sturbridge Village 1290–0111)
* Dark Red Print (R22 Bonnie Blues Basics and Backgrounds 1034–0111)
* Brown Floral (R33 Sturbridge Village IV 1284–0140)

Done

Missouri Puzzle
& Lucy Stone

Born in 1818, Lucy Stone married Henry Blackwell in 1855 but retained her maiden name as a matter of principle. To this day, some women who retain their maiden names after marriage are known as "Lucy Stoners."

Stone was the first woman in Massachusetts to earn a college degree. She worked and studied at the same time because her father refused to pay to educate a woman. After nine years, she had finally saved enough to begin college. Choosing the school was easy—only one college admitted women, Oberlin College in Ohio.

In 1870, she founded the Woman's Journal, the official publication of the American Woman Suffrage Association for nearly 50 years.

Lucy was known for her extraordinary speaking skills and thus became one of the leading advocates of the suffrage movement working for the cause for almost fifty years. Both Susan B. Anthony and Julia Ward Howe credit Stone's speaking as the reason for their conversion to the suffrage movement.

> "'We, the people of the United States.' Which 'we the people?' The women were not included."
>
> LUCY STONE

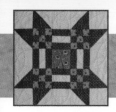

**Fabrics needed
to make Block I**
Background
Red Print
Blue Print
Brown Print

"We want rights.
The flour–merchant,
the house–builder,
and the postman
charge us no less on
account of our sex;
but when we
endeavor to earn
money to pay all
these, then,
indeed, we find
the difference."

LUCY STONE

To Make the Block

Templates for Missouri Puzzle are found on page 90. **Note:** Because of this block's 5x5 grid, we recommend you use the templates to make this block finish to 12".

From the background fabric, cut:
* 8 – 2⅞" A squares (template A)
* 8 – B triangles. Cut 4 – 3¼" squares. Cut each square from corner to corner once on the diagonal or use template B
* 4 – 1¼" x 2⅞" D rectangles (template D)

From the red print cut:
* 8 – B triangles. Cut 4 – 3¼" squares. Cut each square from corner to corner once on the diagonal or use template B
* 16 – 1¼" C squares (template C)
* 8 – 1¼" x 2⅞" D rectangles (template D)

From the blue print cut:
* 20 – 1¼" C squares (template C)

From the brown print cut:
* 1 – 2⅞" A square (template A)

Piecing Directions

* **Note** To make this block finish to 12", it is important to sew units with a scant one-quarter inch seam allowance. Trim each unit to 2⅞" square.

* Make four nine–patch units using the C squares. Alternate the red and blue prints as shown. Trim each unit to 2⅞" square.

* Make 4 pieced squares from the red print and background D rectangles alternating the lights and darks as shown. Trim each unit to 2⅞" square.

* Make 8 half-square triangles pairing a background B triangle with a red print A triangle. Trim each unit to 2⅞" square.

※ Sew the block together in rows as shown.

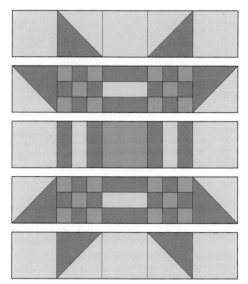

"I think that the young women of today do not and can never know at what price their right to free speech and to speak at all in public has been earned."

LUCY STONE

Centennial Lily
& Amelia Jenks Bloomer

Amelia Jenks was born in New York in 1818. While working as a schoolteacher, she met her husband, Dexter Bloomer, and they wed in 1840. The wedding ceremony was notable in that Jenks declined to include the word "obey" in her vows. Dexter was the editor and publisher of a county newspaper and soon Amelia began writing editorials for the paper, primarily on the subject of temperance or avoiding the excessive use of alcohol.

Bloomer lived in Seneca Falls in 1848 at the time of the women's rights convention but did not actively participate in it. Instead her early work focused almost exclusively on the Temperance Movement. In 1849, Bloomer founded The Lily, a monthly magazine devoted to temperance issues. Through that effort, she met Susan B. Anthony and was actually responsible for introducing Anthony to Elizabeth Cady Stanton, another activist for women's rights. Over time, all three women wrote articles for The Lily and slowly its focus changed from temperance to women's rights.

By 1850, Bloomer's interest had expanded to cover the topic of women's dress. She began wearing loose blouses, short skirts and knee–length, trouser–like undergarments rather than the corsets and long, heavy skirts that were typical during that era. Because she spoke in public frequently on the issue of women's rights, she became associated with the new style of garments and eventually the undergarment took on her name as "bloomers." When other women's rights advocates returned to wearing long skirts because of the ridicule received for the bloomers, Amelia refused to bow to pressure and wore the garments until the late 1850s. By that time, women's attire had changed to include a focus on less restrictive, lighter garments so Bloomer returned to more traditional female attire in order to reduce attention on her clothing and focus discussion on the issues she cared about.

By 1855, Bloomer & her husband moved to Iowa where she became the president of the Iowa Women's Suffrage Society. In this role, she frequently spoke at public gatherings on the topic of the woman's right to vote. Bloomer died in 1894 before realizing the right to vote herself.

"It will not do to say that it is out of woman's sphere to assist in making laws, for if that were so, then it should be also out of her sphere to submit to them."

AMELIA JENKS BLOOMER

**Fabrics needed
to make Block 2**
Background
Red Print
Pink Print
Green Print I
Green Print 2

To Make the Block
Templates for Centennial Lily are found on page 91.

From the background fabric, cut:
❋ 1 – 14" square

From the red print, cut:
❋ 6 – template D

From the pink print, cut:
❋ 9 – template C

From the green print I, cut:
❋ 2 – template B and Br

From the green print 2, cut:
❋ 3 – template A
❋ 27" of ¼" wide bias stems using your preferred method

❋ Refer to the placement diagram and appliqué in place using your favorite method. Trim block to 12½" square after appliqué is complete.

"When you find a burden in belief or apparel, cast it off."

AMELIA JENKS BLOOMER

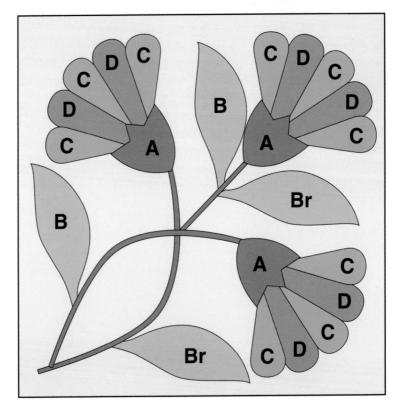

"Although the doctrine of innate equality of the race has been proclaimed, yet so far as woman is concerned it has been a standing falsehood."

AMELIA JENKS BLOOMER

Framed Variable Star
& Mary Church Terrell

Born Sept. 23, 1863, Mary Church Terrell is one of the lesser–known activists for women's equality and the right to vote. In an unusual move for the times, Mary was sent to live with family friends in Ohio so she could attend school. She went on to graduate from Oberlin College, one of the first African–American women to receive a college degree. Against her father's wishes, Mary became a schoolteacher. Because her father believed women should not work, he offered to continue her education in Europe where she spent two years learning languages and enjoying the culture.

Mary married Robert Terrell in 1891, and they made their home in Washington, D.C. Shortly after her marriage, she founded the Colored Woman's League, CWL. In the late 1890s, many local service clubs for black women formed throughout the northern states. However, they were not allowed to affiliate with national organizations like the National Council of Women or the General Federation of Women's Clubs. Frustrated that they could not reach a national audience, the CWL merged with the National Federation of Afro–American Women to become the National Association of Colored Women.

Terrell found that sometimes her support of women's rights was not welcome. In 1913, women marched in Washington D.C. as part of the effort to get Congress to pass an amendment granting women the vote. When Terrell and other African–Americans arrived, they were directed to the back of the parade line–up. Mary Terrell accepted the decision and moved her group to the back.

At other times, Terrell was welcomed, particularly by Susan B. Anthony who frequently invited Terrell to speak at meetings of the National American Woman Suffrage Association. Terrell often used these opportunities to encourage white women to include the cause of racial equality in their efforts. Terrell often argued that justice could not exist until all women were granted equal opportunities and rights.

In 1940, Terrell published her autobiography *A Colored Woman in a White World* which documented the many times she had experienced discrimination and prejudice throughout her life including being denied food in restaurants and being refused rooms in motels. In her late 80s, Mary led efforts to enforce the anti–discrimination laws in Washington, D.C. With a cane in hand, she led many marches and picket lines at area restaurants that would not seat blacks. She successfully sued the city over the issue in 1953 and was at last able to dine & shop throughout the city. Terrell died in 1954 shortly after the landmark Supreme Court decision in *Brown v. Board of Education* mandated desegregation of schools.

"I cannot help wondering sometimes what I might have become and might have done if I had lived in a country which had not circumscribed and handicapped me on account of my race, that had allowed me to reach any height I was able to attain."

MARY CHURCH TERRELL

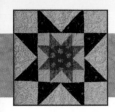
**Fabrics needed
to make Block 3**
Background I
Background 2
Red Print
Green Print
Black Print

"The elective
franchise is withheld
from one half of its
citizens…because the
word 'people,' by
an unparalleled
exhibition of lexicon
graphical acrobatics,
has been turned and
twisted to mean all
who were shrewd and
wise enough to have
themselves born boys
instead of girls, or
who took the trouble
to be born white
instead of black."

MARY CHURCH TERRELL

To Make the Block

Templates for Framed Variable Star are found on page 92.

From background fabric I, cut:
✱ 4 – 3½" squares (template A).
✱ 4 – B triangles. Cut I – 7¼" square. Cut the square from corner to corner on both diagonals or use template B.

From background fabric 2 cut:
✱ 4 – 2" x 2" squares (template E)
✱ 4 – F triangles. Cut I – 4¼" square. Cut the square from corner to corner on both diagonals or use template F.

From the red print cut:
✱ I – 3 ½" square (template A).

From the green print cut:
✱ 8 – D triangles. Cut 4 – 2⅜" squares. Cut each square from corner to corner once on the diagonal or use template D.

From the black print cut:
✱ 8 – C triangles. Cut 4 – 3⅞" squares. Cut each square from corner to corner once on the diagonal or use template C.

Piecing Directions

✱ Sew I C triangle to each short edge of I B triangle to make a large rectangle unit. Repeat to make four units.

✱ Repeat with the 8 – D triangles and 4 – F triangles to make 4 small rectangle units.
✱ Sew 2 small rectangle units to opposite sides of the red A square.

✱ Sew 2 E squares to opposite ends of the remaining 2 small rectangle units.

❋ Sew these units together to form a small star.

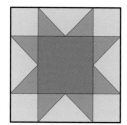

❋ Sew 2 large rectangle units to opposite sides of the small star. Sew 2 A squares to opposite ends of the remaining 2 large rectangle units. Sew these units together to form the large star surrounding the small star.

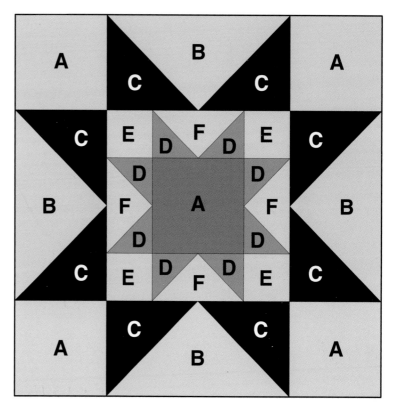

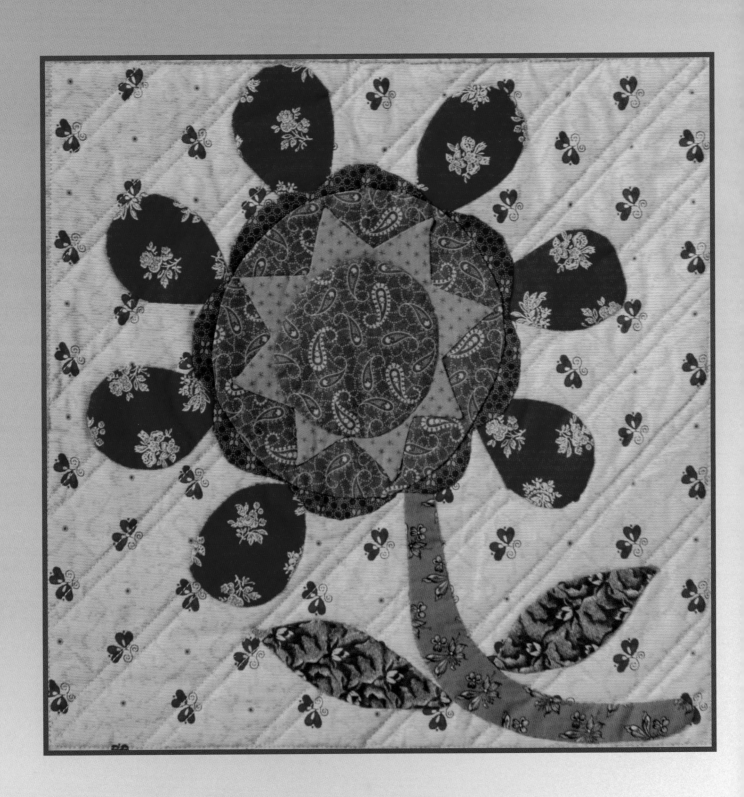

BLOCK 4 • 12" FINISHED

Whig Rose
and Julia Ward Howe

Julia Ward Howe not only is remembered as a women's activist, she fought for the causes of peace and abolition as well. But, she is best remembered today for penning the Battle Hymn of the Republic in 1861. She also is the creator of Mother's Day to promote an official celebration of motherhood and peace.

Born in New York City on May 27, 1819, Julia's mother died when she was 5 years old, leaving her to be raised by a strict father. Despite his reservations, Julia was allowed an extensive education. Julia spent her childhood learning five different languages as well as receiving schooling in math, literature and science. An accomplished writer, Julia had her first manuscripts published anonymously at the age of 20.

Julia's father died in 1839 leaving her a very wealthy heiress. She married Samuel Howe, an abolitionist, in 1843. Howe was 20 years older than Julia and had strong views about the role of women and men in a marriage. He quickly took over all of her inheritance and insisted she stay home as a wife and mother. Julia struggled with this new lifestyle after her years of education and her early success as a writer. In 1852, Julia briefly separated from Samuel. She returned when he threatened to gain custody of their children. However, upon her return, Julia again began publishing articles and poems despite Samuel's protests. When Samuel began publishing an anti–slavery newspaper, *The Commonwealth,* he came to appreciate Julia's literary skills and she assisted him with writing articles and producing the paper. In 1861 she wrote the lyrics for *The Battle Hymn of the Republic* which became an anthem for Union soldiers and remains one of her most recognizable accomplishments.

By 1868, Howe had begun attending meetings of local suffrage associations. She soon began speaking at the events. Then in 1869, she and Lucy Stone organized the American Woman Suffrage Association. This organization differed from the National Woman Suffrage Association (NWSA) because it welcomed men as members and focused solely on suffrage. In contrast, the NWSA wanted to address a variety of issues relating to women including property rights and equal pay issues. She also co–founded the *Woman's Journal* and wrote articles on gender, racial and legal equality for all for more than 20 years.

Howe is also credited with creating the Mother's Day holiday in America. Originally held on the second Sunday in June, Howe promoted the concept of an official celebration of motherhood and peace which would give women a chance to object to wars. Eventually the holiday was recognized nationally and moved to its current date in May.

Howe died in October 1910 before seeing the right to vote for women enacted.

> "I think nothing is religion which puts one individual absolutely above others, and surely nothing is religion which puts one sex above another."
>
> JULIA WARD HOWE

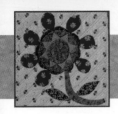

Whig Rose continued

**Fabric needed
to make Block 4:**
Background
Red Print
Pink Print
Blue Print
Brown Print
Green Print I
Green Print 2

"Marriage, like
death, is a debt we
owe to nature."

JULIA WARD HOWE

To Make the Block
Templates for Whig Rose are found on page 93.

From the background fabric, cut:
✳ I – 14" square

From the red print, cut:
✳ 7 – template E

From the pink print, cut:
✳ 8 – template C

From the blue print, cut:
✳ I - template A
✳ I - template B

From the brown print, cut:
✳ I – template D

From the green print I, cut:
✳ 9" of ½" wide bias stem using your preferred method

From the green print 2 cut:
✳ 2 – template F

✳ Refer to the placement diagram and appliqué in place using your favorite method.
Trim block to 12½" square after appliqué is complete.

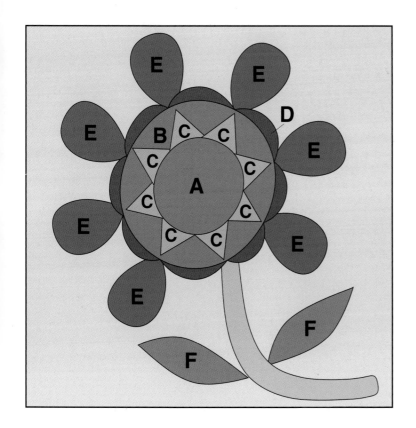

"Any religion which sacrifices
women to the brutality of men
is no religion."

JULIA WARD HOWE

Four X
& Jane Addams

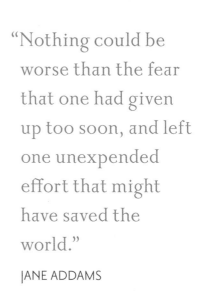

B orn in 1860 in Cedarville, Illinois, Jane's family was well–off and encouraged her to pursue an education. After graduating from Rockford Seminary, Jane toured Europe for a year while considering her future. When she returned home, her father became ill and died. Jane worried that her ambitious career goals, including a medical degree, had created stress for her father, leading to his death.

In 1888 Jane returned to Europe with her friend, Ellen Starr, and in addition to sight–seeing, they toured Toynbee Hall, a settlement house created to help those living in the slums in London. Upon their return, Jane and Ellen decided to start a similar house in Chicago. Jane envisioned a place where young, educated women who did not want to marry and stay at home could have an active role in society.

Soon, Jane's creation, Hull House, helped the poor with vocational skills, food, shelter, medical care and child care. By 1893 Hull House served more than 2,000 people a week. The house provided education and cultural opportunities to a community that would have no other opportunity to experience art or music.

Jane soon decided that the best way to end poverty was to attack its root causes. To that end, she began lobbying government for changes to labor laws, factory work conditions and equality issues. This idea that government should have policies on topics like public health and safety, the conduct of businesses and housing standards was the foundation of the Progressive Movement, a political force from 1900 to 1920. Jane's political involvement led her to the suffrage movement. Many of the causes championed by the Progressive Movement such as restrictions on child labor were issues important to women. Naturally, then, the suffrage movement became aligned with the Progressive Movement as women sought a stronger voice in their government.

In 1915 Addams became chair of the Women's Peace Party and president of the International Congress of Women, both organizations designed to lobby against world wars. She led meetings at The Hague arguing that the United States and other countries should not join in World War I. Throughout all of these efforts, Addams continued her work with Hull House and it served thousands of people as economic conditions worsened. Her anti–war efforts were very unpopular and for a while Jane was ridiculed as a peacenik and "Bolshevik."

Jane continued her hard work on the issues she cared about including world peace despite public criticism. Ultimately, her work was rewarded in 1931 when she became the first woman to win a Nobel Peace Prize for her tireless efforts to improve conditions for her fellow man and her work on behalf of peace.

"Nothing could be worse than the fear that one had given up too soon, and left one unexpended effort that might have saved the world."

JANE ADDAMS

**Fabrics needed
to make Block 5**
Background Print
Brown Print
Blue Print

To Make the Block
Templates for Four X are found on page 94. **Note:** Because of this block's
5x5 grid, we recommend you use the templates to make this block finish to 12".

From the background print, cut:
- ❋ 8 – 2⅞" squares (template A).
- ❋ 8 – B triangles. Cut 4 – 3¼" squares. Cut each square from corner to corner once on the diagonal or use template B.

From the brown print, cut:
- ❋ 5 – 2⅞" squares (template A).
- ❋ 8 – B triangles. Cut 4 – 3¼" squares. Cut each square from corner to corner once on the diagonal or use template B.

From the blue print, cut:
- ❋ 4 – 2⅞" squares (template A).

Piecing Directions
- ❋ **Note** To make this block come out to 12" finished, it's important to sew all seams using a scant ¼" seam allowance.
- ❋ Stitch each background B triangle to a brown B triangle to make 8 half–square triangles.

- ❋ Referring to the diagram, layout the block in rows and sew each unit together.
- ❋ Make 2 rows like this:

- ❋ Make 2 rows like this:

- ❋ Then, make 1 row like this:

"Old–fashioned ways
which no longer
apply to changed
conditions are a
snare in which the
feet of women have
always become
readily entangled."

JANE ADDAMS

✽ Referring to the diagram rotate the rows to match the picture. Sew the rows together to form the block.

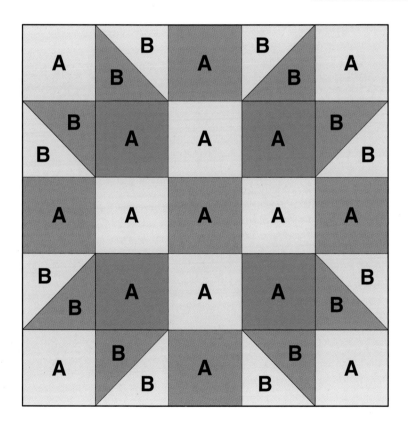

"I do not believe that women are better than men. We have not wrecked railroads, nor corrupted legislatures, nor done many unholy things that men have done; but then we must remember that we have not had the chance."

JANE ADDAMS

Love Apple
& Elizabeth Cady Stanton

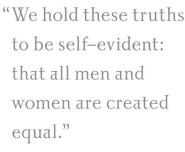

Born November 12, 1815, Elizabeth Cady Stanton was a significant part of the suffrage movement who often operated behind the scenes. Her father Daniel Cady, was a lawyer and taught Elizabeth at home in addition to her studies at Troy Female Seminary. When Elizabeth's brother died, her father exclaimed "Oh my daughter I wish you were a boy". Cady decided then to make her father proud of her by excelling in her studies and other male pursuits.

Cady married Harry Stanton, a leader in the anti–slavery effort, in 1840. Shortly after the marriage, they attended the World Anti–Slavery Conference in London. Denied a seat at the conference because she was female, Elizabeth was outraged and decided it was time to take action. She met Lucretia Mott at the conference, who was also denied a seat, and began a discussion of what women needed to do in order to gain equality.

By 1848, Stanton organized the Seneca Falls Convention, the first formal event calling for women's rights. Stanton authored the Declaration of Sentiments, which officially started the struggle for the right to vote. Stanton insisted on including suffrage as part of the platform even though the idea was opposed by both her husband and Mott.

In 1851, Stanton began working with Susan B. Anthony. For many years thereafter, Anthony devised the strategy of the effort while Stanton wrote out policies and articles. When the Reconstruction efforts following the Civil War only granted freed male slaves the right to vote, the two women decided to create the National American Woman Suffrage Association. Stanton served as its first president. Stanton and Anthony worked together until their disagreement on a fundamental issue fractured their alliance. Anthony believed that obtaining the vote would allow women to fix all the wrongs in society. In contrast, Stanton wanted to address issues like discriminatory divorce and property laws that harmed women and believed that once those issues were corrected, the right to vote would naturally follow.

Stanton also drew criticism for her attacks on religion. She firmly believed that religion was designed by men to keep women uneducated and in the home. Eventually, she wrote a two–volume work called *The Woman's Bible* summarizing her thoughts on organized religion. The book was very controversial but remains in print to this day as a feminist critique of the Bible.

Stanton had 7 children and one of her joys was seeing her daughter, Harriot, graduate from Vassar College in 1878. Stanton died in 1902 before gaining the right to vote.

> "We hold these truths to be self–evident: that all men and women are created equal."
>
> ELIZABETH CADY STANTON

**Fabrics needed
to make Block 6**
Background
Red Print 1
Red Print 2
Red Print 3
Green Print
Gold Print

"The happiest people
I have known have
been those who gave
themselves no
concern about their
own souls, but did
their uttermost to
mitigate the miseries
of others."

ELIZABETH CADY STANTON

To Make the Block
Templates for Love Apple are found on page 95.

From the background fabric, cut:
❋ 1 – 14" square

From red print 1, cut:
❋ 1 - template A
❋ 1 – template E and Er

From red print 2, cut:
❋ 1 – template C

From red print 3, cut:
❋ 1 – template B

From the green print, cut:
❋ 1 – template F and Fr
❋ 9" of ½" wide bias stems using your preferred method

From gold print cut:
❋ 1 – template D

❋ Refer to the placement diagram and appliqué in place using your favorite method. Trim block to 12½" after appliqué is complete.

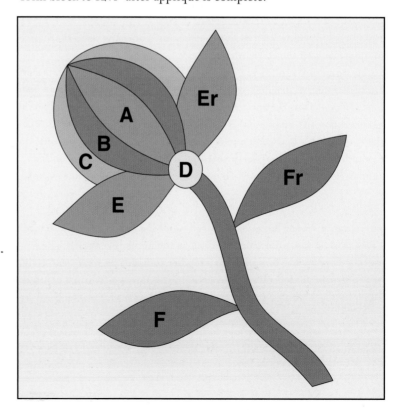

"Because man and woman are the complement of one another, we need woman's thought in national affairs to make a safe and stable government."

ELIZABETH CADY STANTON

Log Cabin & Sojourner Truth

Isabella Baumfree, also known as Sojourner Truth, was born a slave in 1797 and one of 13 children. Isabella was sold, along with a herd of sheep, to a new master at age 9 for $100. By the age of 18, Isabella had been sold twice more ending up with John Dumont. Isabella was forced to marry a fellow slave, Thomas. Together, they had 5 children.

Isabella eventually escaped from Dumont with her infant daughter, Sofia. The Van Wegenen family took her in and helped her regain custody of a 5-year-old son who had been traded away. While living with the Van Wegenen's she had an intense religious experience and began preaching. In 1843 she changed her name to Sojourner Truth and began working as a traveling preacher. During her travels, she met William Lloyd Garrison, who published her memoirs *The Narrative of Sojourner Truth: A Northern Slave.*

In 1854, Sojourner appeared at the Ohio Woman's Rights Convention and gave her most famous speech, *Ain't I a Woman?* The speech inspired both anti-slavery and women's rights advocates with this particularly poignant passage:

"That man over there says that women need to be helped into carriages, and lifted over ditches, and to have the best place everywhere. Nobody ever helps me into carriages, or over mud puddles, or gives me any best place, and ain't I a woman?...I have plowed, and planted, and gathered into barns, and no man could head me—and ain't I a woman? I could work as much and eat as much as a man (when I could get it), and bear the lash as well—and ain't I a woman? I have borne thirteen children and seen most all sold off to slavery and when I cried out with my mother's grief, none but Jesus heard me—and ain't I woman?"

After the Civil War, Sojourner expanded her work to include property rights for freed slaves. For years, she lobbied Congress to give former slaves free land in the West. Her efforts were largely ignored. She continued traveling and speaking, primarily at churches until her death in 1883.

"Where did your Christ come from? From God and a woman! Man had nothing to do with Him."

SOJOURNER TRUTH

**Fabric needed
to make Block 7**
Black
Light Brown Print I
Medium Brown Print 2
Dark Brown Print 3
Light Red Print I
Medium Red Print 2
Dark Red Print 3

To Make the Block
Templates are not provided for Log Cabin block; however, you can easily make your own by using the dimensions given below for each rectangle.

From black, cut:
❋ I – 3½" square (A).

From light brown print I, cut:
❋ I – 2" x 3½" rectangle (B).
❋ I – 2" x 5" rectangle (C).

From medium brown print 2, cut:
❋ I – 2" x 6½" rectangle (F).
❋ I – 2" x 8" rectangle (G).

From dark brown print 3, cut:
❋ I – 2" x 9½" rectangle (J).
❋ I – 2" x II" rectangle (K).

From light red print I, cut:
❋ I – 2" x 5" rectangle (D).
❋ I – 2" x 6½" rectangle (E).

From medium red print 2 cut:
❋ I – 2" x 8" rectangle (H).
❋ I – 2" x 9½" rectangle (I).

From dark red print 3, cut:
❋ I – 2" x II" rectangle (L).
❋ I – 2" x 12½" rectangle (M).

"There is a great stir about colored men getting their rights, but not a word about the colored women; and if colored men get their rights, and not colored women theirs, you see the colored men will be masters over the women, and it will be just as bad as it was before. So I am for keeping the thing going while things are stirring; because if we wait till it is still, it will take a great while to get it going again."

SOJOURNER TRUTH

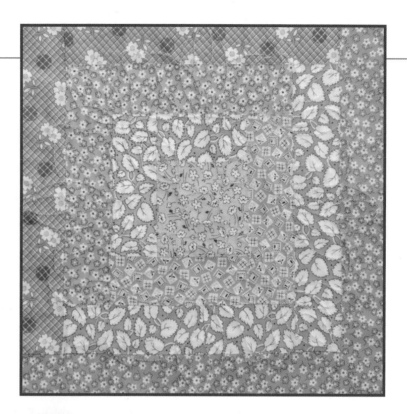

Piecing Directions:

✳ Sew light brown print 1 (B) to the top of the black square (A). Next, sew light brown print 1 (C) to the left side of this unit. Continue working around the square with the next rectangle, light red print 1 (D) and so forth, in alphabetical order, until the block is complete and matches the diagram.

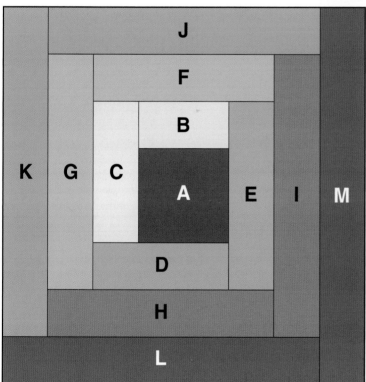

Done

Tulips
& Lucretia Mott

Lucretia Coffin was born into a Quaker family in 1793. Her Massachusetts community practiced equality for all. However, after taking a teaching position at a Quaker school, Lucretia discovered that the female teachers were paid half of the amount paid to male teachers. This sparked her interest in women's rights issues.

After marrying James Mott in 1811, Lucretia discovered a talent for public speaking and began preaching in 1818. She was formally recognized as a Quaker minister in 1821. She opposed slavery and soon began using her ministry skills to deliver anti-slavery speeches.

In 1840, she attended the World Anti-Slavery Convention in London. When organizers refused to seat her and other women as recognized delegates, she met Elizabeth Cady Stanton, and the two began discussing women's rights when they were left in a segregated, women-only seating area. In 1848, Mott and Stanton convened the Seneca Falls Convention which specifically called for equal rights for women.

As a Quaker, Mott struggled with the Civil War. Her belief in non-violent efforts to resolve conflict clashed with her desire to end slavery. In the end, she decided ending slavery was the more important goal.

Following the end of the Civil War, Mott served as president of the American Equal Rights Convention and worked to ease conflict between groups which wanted to focus on black male suffrage before women's suffrage and groups which believed the right to vote should be extended to all people at the same time.

Mott's last public appearance occurred when she was 85. She spoke at a 30-year anniversary celebration of the Seneca Falls Convention. Like many other key activists, Mott never got to cast a vote of her own. However, her efforts were critical to the ultimate success of suffrage.

"The world has never yet seen a truly great and virtuous nation, because in the degradation of women the very fountains of life are poisoned at their source."

LUCRETIA MOTT

**Fabrics needed
to make Block 8**
Background
Red Print 1
Red Print 2
Green Print 1
Green Print 2

To Make the Block
Templates for Tulips are found on page 96.

From the background fabric, cut:
❋ 1 – 14" square

From red print 1, cut:
❋ 3 - template C and Cr

From red print 2, cut:
❋ 3 – template A

From green print 1, cut:
❋ 3 – template B and Br
❋ 3 – template D

From green print 2, cut:
❋ 2 – template E
❋ 1 – template Er
❋ 12" of ½" wide bias stems using your preferred method

❋ Refer to the placement diagram and appliqué in place using your favorite method. Trim block to 12½" after appliqué is complete.

"If our principles are right, why should we be cowards?"

LUCRETIA MOTT

"We too often bind ourselves by authorities rather than by the truth."

LUCRETIA MOTT

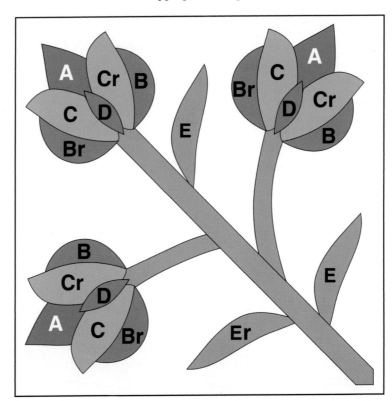

"Learning, while at school, that the charge for
the education of girls was the same as that for
boys, and that, when they became teachers,
women received only half as much as men for
their services, the injustice of this distinction
was so apparent."

LUCRETIA MOTT

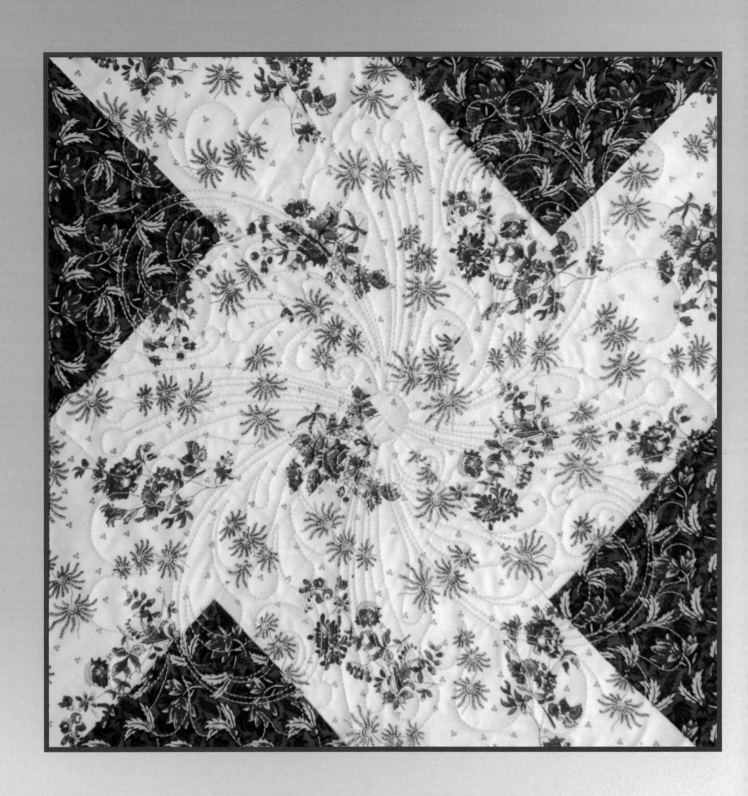

Whirlwind
& Frances Perkins

Frances Perkins was born in 1880 in Boston. Her family was religious and encouraged her to "live for God, and do something." While attending college at Mount Holyoke, Frances came to understand what that meant. Exposure to living conditions in the slums of New York convinced her that she needed to work for social causes.

After graduating, Perkins worked in several settlement houses which provided a variety of services to factory workers. Then, Frances pursued a master's degree in economics and sociology at Columbia University, graduating in 1910. While in New York, she successfully lobbied the New York legislature for a bill that limited the work hours of women and children. At the same time, she discovered the suffrage movement and began speaking on street corners, urging people to support the women's right to vote.

Frances acknowledged that a life-changing moment occurred when she witnessed the Triangle Shirtwaist factory fire. Poor conditions at the factory doomed 146 workers, mostly young women, to their deaths. Frances commented that the fire was "a never-to-be-forgotten reminder of why I had to spend my life fighting conditions that could permit such a tragedy."

By 1918, the governor of New York appointed her to the New York State Industrial Commission, a first for a female. By 1933, she had gained the attention of President Roosevelt who appointed her as Labor Secretary, the first time a woman served in a presidential cabinet. Perkins successfully lobbied for significant reforms on many labor and employment issues.

Perkins continued as Labor Secretary until 1945 when Roosevelt died. President Truman then appointed her to the Civil Service Commission where she continued her work on labor and employment issues. At age 77, Frances joined the Cornell University faculty and taught courses until her death at age 85 in 1965.

"Being a woman has only bothered me in climbing trees."

FRANCES PERKINS

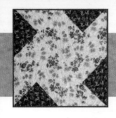

**Fabrics needed
to make Block 9**
Background Print
Brown Print

To Make the Block

Templates for Whirlwind are found on page 97.

From background print, cut:

❋ 4 – shapes using Template A.

From brown print, cut:

❋ 1 – 7¼" square. Cut in half on both diagonals to make 4 triangles (B). Or use Template B.

Piecing Directions:

❋ Sew a Background Print shape A to a Triangle B, sewing along the short edge of both pieces as shown. Repeat to make 4 units.

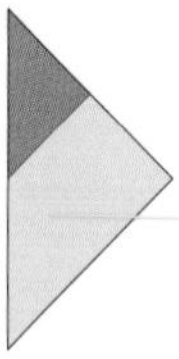

❋ Sew 2 of the units together to form a large triangle as shown. Repeat with remaining 2 units.

❋ Sew the 2 triangles together to form the block.

"The door might not be opened to a woman again for a long, long time, and I had a kind of duty to other women to walk in and sit down on the chair that was offered, and so establish the right of others long hence and far distant in geography to sit in the high seats."

FRANCES PERKINS

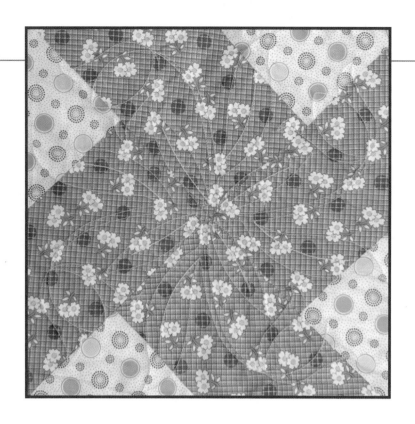

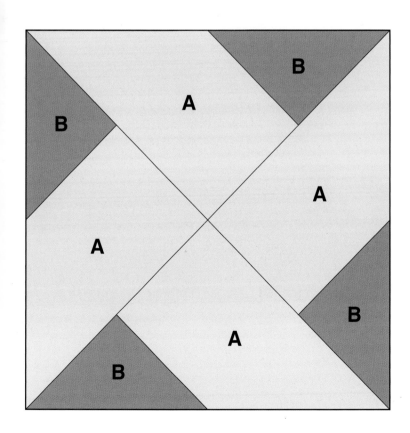

King's Crown
& Fanny Jackson-Coppin

Fanny Jackson-Coppin was born into a life of slavery on October 15, 1837. Fanny's aunt, Sarah Orr Clark purchased her when she was 12. At age 14, Fanny went to work as a housekeeper for George & Mary Calvert. Although she was an employee, the Calverts treated Fanny like a daughter and allowed her to pursue an education.

By 1860, Fanny was ready to enroll in Oberlin College in Ohio. There, she taught reading and writing freed slaves. She was so successful that Oberlin College hired her to teach on the condition that if any students objected to having a black teacher, she would be let go. No one had a problem with Fanny and she was soon teaching three classes at Oberlin.

In 1865, the Institute for Colored Youth offered Fanny a position as a high school teacher. Within a year, she was promoted to principal of its Ladies Department, the first African-American school principal in the country. Then, in 1869, she was promoted to principal of the entire school.

Fanny met a minister, Bishop Levi Jenkins Coppin in 1879 and married him in 1881.

Jackson-Coppin also began writing for area newspapers. Her writings focused on the need for education and encouraged women to enter the workforce. During her time as principal of the Institute, 668 students graduated and a passed a rigorous certification test. These students went on to become the leaders of African-American Society in the United States.

In 1902, Fanny and her husband travelled to South Africa and opened the Bethel Institute, a school devoted to teaching self-help techniques to local citizens. She continued this missionary work for 10 years until her health declined. She returned to the United States and died in 1913. Her significant contributions to education were recognized with the creation of Coppin State College in Baltimore, Maryland.

"Good manners will often take people where neither money nor education will take them."

FANNY JACKSON-COPPIN

**Fabrics needed
to make Block 10**
Background 1 Print
Background 2 Print
Gold Print
Red 1 Print
Red 2 Print
Brown 1 Print
Brown 2 Print

To Make the Block
Templates for King's Crown are found on page 98.

From the background print 1, cut:
※ 8 – B triangles. Cut 4 – 2⅞" squares. Cut each square from corner to corner once on the diagonal or use template B.
※ 4 – C triangles. Cut 1 – 5¼" square. Cut each square from corner to corner twice on each diagonal or use template C.

From the background print 2, cut:
※ 1 – 6⅛" square (template E).

From the gold print, cut:
※ 4 – 2½" squares (template A).

From the red print 1, cut:
※ 4 – B triangles. Cut 2 – 2⅞" squares. Cut each square from corner to corner once on the diagonal or use template B.
※ 1 – D triangle. Cut 1 – 4⅞" square. Cut the square from corner to corner once on the diagonal or use template D. Discard the extra triangle.

From the red print 2, cut:
※ 4 – B triangles. Cut 2 – 2⅞" squares. Cut each square from corner to corner once on the diagonal or use template B.
※ 1 – D triangle. Cut 1 – 4⅞" square. Cut the square from corner to corner once on the diagonal or use template D. Discard the extra triangle.

From the brown print 1, cut:
※ 4 – B triangles. Cut 2 – 2⅞" squares. Cut each square from corner to corner once on the diagonal or use template B.
※ 1 – D triangle. Cut 1 – 4⅞" square. Cut the square from corner to corner once on the diagonal or use template D. Discard the extra triangle.

From the brown print 2, cut:
※ 4 – B triangles. Cut 2 – 2⅞" squares. Cut each square from corner to corner once on the diagonal or use template B.
※ 1 – D triangle. Cut 1 – 4⅞" square. Cut the square from corner to corner once on the diagonal or use template D. Discard the extra triangle.

Piecing Directions
※ Stitch each background 1 B triangle to 2 red print 1 B triangles to make 2 half-square triangle units. Repeat with the red print 2, brown print 1 and brown print 2 to form 2 half-square triangles of each color combination for a total of 8 half-square triangle units.

❋ Stitch a red print #1 B triangle and a brown print #1 B triangle to opposite sides of a background #1 C triangle to form 1 flying geese unit. Refer to the block diagram for proper placement of the red and brown prints. **Note:** Proper color placement is important for the success of this block.

❋ Repeat with the remaining red and brown B triangles and C background print triangles to form a total of 4 flying geese units.

❋ Referring to the block diagram for color placement, stitch the four red and brown Piece D triangles to the background #2 E square. **Note:** Again, pay close attention to color placement for this unit.

❋ Matching the correct reds and browns together, sew a half-square triangle unit to each side of the flying geese unit. Refer to the diagram to ensure that triangles are pointing in the correct direction. Repeat with remaining half-square triangle units and flying geese units to make 4 units.

❋ Stitch two of these rows to opposite sides of the large pieced square, making sure fabrics match.

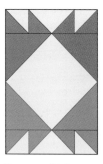

❋ Sew 2 gold A squares to opposite ends of the two remaining rows.

✳ Sew these rows to opposite sides of the pieced unit to complete the block.

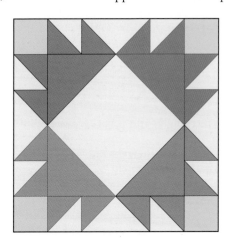

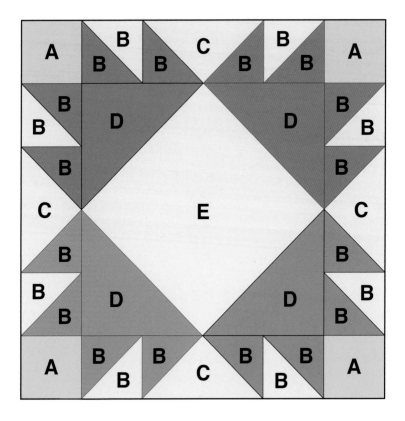

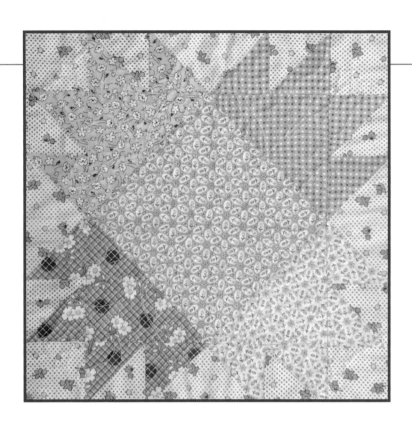

"We should strive to make known to all men the justice of our claims to the same employment as other men under the same conditions. We do not ask that any one of our people shall be put in a position because he is a colored person, but we do ask that he shall not be kept out of a position because he is a colored person. 'An open field and no favors' is all that is requested."

FANNY JACKSON-COPPIN

Oak Leaves & Flowers
& Susan B. Anthony

Born into a strict Quaker family on Feb. 15, 1820, Susan Brownell Anthony was taught to believe in herself and her convictions at an early age. Her parents sent her to school but the teachers refused to instruct her in things like math because that was not a subject taught to women at the time. Her father arranged for private schooling for Susan and her sisters using a female teacher which first gave Susan the idea that women could do something other than be a wife and mother.

After finishing her schooling, Susan returned to the family home in Rochester. Her family attended the Seneca Falls Convention where both of her parents and a sister signed the Declaration of Sentiments calling for equal rights for women. She believed that women suffered when their husbands were alcoholics so she created the Women's State Temperance Society in 1849 in part because she was prohibited from speaking at public rallies against alcohol because she was a woman.

While leading the Temperance Society, Anthony organized a petition drive to call on New York state legislators to ban the sale of alcohol. The legislators rejected her request when they reviewed the petitions and noted that of the 28,000 signatures gathered, most were from women and children. This experience convinced Anthony that women would only gain a voice in society when they had the right to vote. Feeling that the issues of voting and equality of all citizens were the most important causes of the day, Susan resigned from the Temperance Society and devoted her work to the American Anti-Slavery Society from 1854 to 1861.

Following the Civil War, Anthony was outraged that black males had received rights under the 14th and 15th Amendments to the U.S. Constitution which were not extended to white women. This included the right to vote. She tried to vote in elections in both 1872 and 1873 and was arrested and convicted both times. However, she refused to pay any fines associated with the convictions and the courts did not enforce the fines so that she would not have grounds to appeal and have the suffrage issue decided by a higher court.

Anthony died in 1906 before gaining the right to vote for herself. Her dedication and commitment to the suffrage movement, however, undoubtedly helped gain the right to vote for women. In 1920, fourteen years after her death, her original amendment was adopted as the 19th Amendment to the United States Constitution.

> "There never will be complete equality until women themselves help to make laws and elect lawmakers."
> SUSAN B. ANTHONY

**Fabrics needed
to make Block II**
Background
Black Print
Red Print
Blue Print
Gold Print

"It was we, the
people; not we, the
white male citizens;
nor yet we, the male
citizens; but we, the
whole people, who
formed the Union."

SUSAN B. ANTHONY

To Make the Block

Templates for Oak Leaves and Flowers are found on page 99.

From the background fabric, cut:
❋ 1 – 14" square

From the black print, cut:
❋ 1 - template A

From the red print, cut:
❋ 2 – template B
❋ 4 – template D
❋ 1 – template G

From the blue print, cut:
❋ 2 – template B
❋ 2 – template C
❋ 1 – template F

From the gold, cut:
❋ 2 – template C
❋ 4 – template D
❋ 1 – template E

❋ To create template A, fold a 12" square piece of freezer paper in half and in half again. Open up the paper and trace the template onto one quarter of the freezer paper, being sure to line up the center of the paper with the point on the template. Refold the freezer paper and cut on the drawn line.

❋ Cut out the appliqué shapes, adding ⅛" to ¼" seam allowance. Press the background in half vertically, then again horizontally to find the center of the background fabric. Refer to the placement diagram and appliqué in place using your favorite method. Trim block to 12½" square after appliqué is complete.

"Cautious, careful people, always casting about to preserve their reputation and social standing, never can bring about a reform. Those who are really in earnest must be willing to be anything or nothing in the world's estimation, and publicly and privately, in season and out, avow their sympathy with despised and persecuted ideas and their advocates, and bear the consequences."

SUSAN B. ANTHONY

New York Beauty
& Carrie Chapman Catt

Born in 1859, Carrie Lane focused on education from an early age attending a one-room schoolhouse in Iowa when many young girls did not. At age 13, Carrie asked the family why her mother did not go into town to vote when her father did. The family reacted with laughter saying that voting was too important to be left to women. This event would shape Carrie's future work as she believed women were equal to men.

By 1880 she had worked her way through Iowa State College, graduating at the top of her class. In 1883 she was one of the first women in the country to be appointed superintendent of schools. She married Leo Chapman in 1885 but he died a year later of typhoid fever. In 1887 she began working for the Iowa Woman Suffrage Association as a writer and speaker. While working on suffrage issues, she met George Catt who encouraged her efforts. They married in 1890 and Carrie began working for the National American Woman Suffrage Association (NAWSA).

Catt's speaking abilities were renowned and in 1892 Susan B. Anthony selected Catt to deliver an address to Congress on suffrage. She also organized the International Woman Suffrage Alliance that year which brought together women's rights organizations from 32 countries.

Catt returned to lead the NAWSA in 1915 and developed a "Winning Plan" to push for suffrage on the state and federal levels simultaneously while accepting partial suffrage in states that were extremely resistant to giving women the vote. With her leadership, Congress finally embraced the suffrage concept and President Woodrow Wilson also added his support. The 19th Amendment became part of the Constitution on Aug. 26, 1920.

Following adoption of the amendment, Catt founded the League of Women Voters, an organization which exists to this day. The League works to educate voters about candidates and issues in elections each year. Carrie died in 1947 leaving a lasting legacy for women in the United States.

"Do not stand in the way of the next step in human progress. No one living who reads the signs of the times but realizes that woman suffrage must come. We are working for the ballot as a matter of justice and as a step for human betterment."

CARRIE CHAPMAN CATT

**Fabrics needed
to make Block 12**

Background Print

Light Red Print

Dark Red Print

Brown Floral

To Make the Block

Templates for New York Beauty are found on pages 100-101.

From the light red print, cut:

❋ I – template A. Fold the fabric in half. Matching the fold line on template A with the fold line of the fabric, trace the template and cut out one shape.

From the background print, cut:

❋ 4 – B triangles (template B)

❋ I – D triangle (template D & Dr)

❋ I – Dr triangle (template D & Dr)

From the dark red print, cut:

❋ 5 – C triangles (template C)

From the brown floral, cut:

❋ I – E shape (template E)

Piecing Directions

❋ Lay out the B, C, D and Dr pieces as shown in the diagram. Stitch the D triangle to a C triangle. Gently press being careful not to stretch the bias. Sew a B triangle to this unit. Alternate the C triangles with B triangles until you come to the last C triangle. Sew the Dr triangle to the end of the row and press.

❋ To attach the A and E shape to the pieced arc, you will need to do some curved piecing. First fold the units in half and make a small dot at the center point of each piece. If you pin the pieces properly, you can easily do this by machine. Always put the convex (hill-shaped) piece on the bottom. Gently lay the concave piece on top, right sides together. Pin the pieces together at each end.

❋ Line up the centers of Piece A and the outer edge of the crown points and pin together. Work with one-half of the unit at a time. Smooth the concave edge along the convex curve until the edges are aligned. Pin approximately every I". You may need to clip a few spots in the concave piece, but this is a gentle curve and we were able to piece this without clipping. If you do clip, make sure you only clip in the seam allowance, not your actual block piece.

❋ Sew using a one-quarter-inch seam allowance to the center point of the two units. Lower the machine needle into the center point. Gently align the concave edge with the convex edge of the pieces for the remaining half of the unit. Pin and clip as before. Sew to the end of the unit. Press gently so everything lays flat. Repeat the process to sew piece E to the inner edge of the crown points.

Paper Piecing Instructions

If you choose to paper piece the crown points section, use the paper piecing diagram found on pages 102-103.

"The world taught women nothing skillful and then said her work was valueless. It permitted her no opinions and said she did not know how to think. It forbade her to speak in public and said the sex had no orators. It denied her the schools, and said the sex had no genius. It robbed her of every vestige of responsibility, and then called her weak. It taught her that every pleasure must come as a favor from men and when, to gain it, she decked herself in paint and fine feathers, as she had been taught to do, it called her vain."

CARRIE CHAPMAN CATT

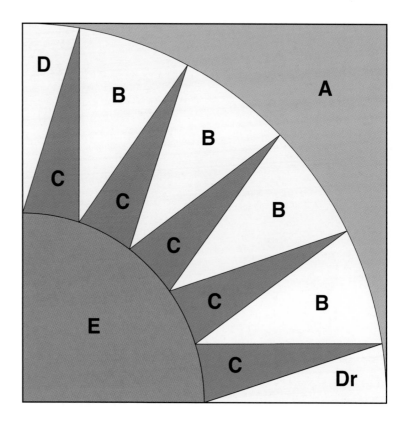

89" X 104"

Rhubarb Crisp

MADE BY SARAH MAXWELL • QUILTED BY CONNIE GRESHAM

Using the Four X block with a scrappy but controlled color scheme, Sarah created a quilt she's always wanted. The classic 1800s color combination of double pink and chocolate brown has long been a favorite of Sarah's. So, she combined a variety of these colors along with two shirting-style backgrounds to create this quilt. Large blocks make the piecing quick so you can have a bed-sized quilt in a short time.

To Make the Quilt

Rhubarb Crisp includes 30 – 15" finished blocks. Fifteen of the blocks are primarily pink; the other fifteen are primarily brown. Two background prints are used to further highlight the difference between the pink and brown blocks.

Cutting for one pink block:

A	B/B	A	B/B	A
B/B	A	A	A	B/B
A	A	A	A	A
B/B	A	A	A	B/B
A	B/B	A	B/B	A

Fabrics

2 yards of light background print #1
2 yards of light background print #2
2¼ yards total of assorted brown prints
2¼ yards total of assorted pink prints
⅝ yard of medium brown for inner border
1⅞ yards of pink and brown stripe for outer border
⅞ yard of dark brown for binding
8¼ yards for backing

From light background print #1, cut:
❋ 8 – 3½" squares (A).
❋ 4 – 3⅞" squares. Cut each in half on the diagonal to form 8 triangles (B).

From one pink print, cut:
❋ 5 – 3½" squares (A).
❋ 4 – 3⅞" squares. Cut each in half on the diagonal to form 8 triangles (B).

From one brown print, cut:
❋ 4 – 3½" squares (A).

Piecing for one pink block
❋ Make 8 half-square triangles by stitching each pink triangle (B) to each background print #1 triangle (B). Press to the pink.

Make 8

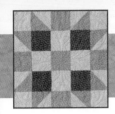
✳ Referring to the diagrams, lay out the units in rows and sew together. On the odd-numbered rows (I, 3, 5), press the seams toward the left. On the even-numbered rows (2, 4), press the seams toward the right. The seams will be going in opposite directions when the rows are sewn together helping the block lay flat.

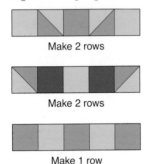

Make 2 rows

Make 2 rows

Make 1 row

✳ Referring to the block diagram, rotate the rows to match the picture. Join the rows together to form the block. Press seams in one direction.

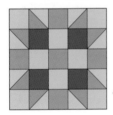

✳ Make a total of 15 pink blocks, varying the browns and pinks in each block to achieve the scrappy look shown.

Cutting for one brown block:
From light background print #2, cut:
✳ 8 – 3½" squares (A).
✳ 4 – 3⅞" squares. Cut each in half on the diagonal to form 8 triangles (B).

From one brown print, cut:
✳ 5 – 3½" squares (A).
✳ 4 – 3⅞" squares. Cut each in half on the diagonal to form 8 triangles (B).

From one pink print, cut:
✳ 4 – 3½" squares (A).

Piecing for one brown block:
✳ Make 8 half-square triangles by stitching each brown triangle (B) to each background print #2 triangle (B). Press to the brown.

Make 8

✳ Referring to the diagrams, lay out the units in rows and sew together. On the odd-numbered rows (I, 3, 5), press the seams toward the left. On the even-numbered rows (2, 4), press the seams toward the right. The seams will be going in opposite directions when the rows are sewn together helping the block lay flat.

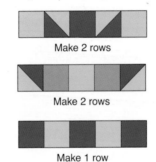

Make 2 rows

Make 2 rows

Make 1 row

✳ Referring to the block diagram rotate the rows to match the picture. Join the rows together to form the block. Press seams in one direction.

✳ Make a total of 15 brown blocks, varying the browns and pinks in each block to achieve the scrappy look shown.

Quilt Top Assembly

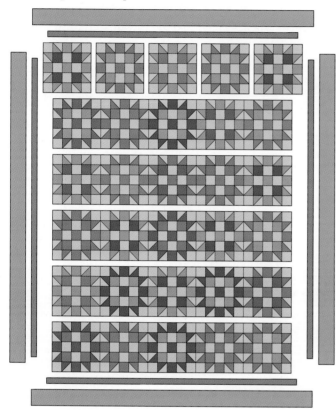

✳ Lay out the 30 blocks alternating pink blocks with brown blocks as shown in the assembly diagram. Sew the quilt together in 5 rows of 6 blocks each.

Borders

Inner border
From the inner border print, cut:

✳ 9 – 2" strips x the width of the fabric.

✳ Measure your quilt top from top to bottom through the center. Piece together inner border strips to make 2 strips equal to this measurement. Sew the strips on each side of the quilt.

✳ Measure your quilt top again from side to side through the center. Piece together inner border strips to make 2 strips equal to this measurement. Sew the strips to the top and bottom of the quilt.

Outer border
From the outer border print, cut:

✳ 10 – 6" strips x the width of the fabric.

✳ Measure your quilt top from top to bottom through the center. Piece together outer border strips to make 2 strips equal to this measurement. Sew the strips on each side of the quilt.

✳ Measure your quilt top again from side to side through the center. Piece together outer border strips to make 2 strips equal to this measurement. Sew the strips to the top and bottom of the quilt.

Finishing
Quilt as desired.

✳ From the binding fabric, cut 10 – 2½" wide strips. Piece strips together to make a continuous binding strip.

95" X 95"

Starry Nights

MADE BY SARAH MAXWELL · QUILTED BY CONNIE GRESHAM

Using the Framed Variable Star block as a beginning, Sarah added half-square triangles instead of the plain squares at the corners of the block and continued framing the star with flying geese units to make this 92" square quilt perfect for a bed. Simple, large pieces are perfect for showcasing your favorite prints. The easy piecing means you can complete this top in a weekend.

To Make the Quilt

Starry Nights starts with a center Framed Variable Star block. Star points in gradated sizes surround this center block. The gradated star points are created by adding Rounds of pieced strips to the center star. Begin by making the center star. Then add Round 2, Round 3 and Round 4. Two borders complete the quilt top.

Note: Because of the large pieces in this quilt that are cut on the bias, it's a good idea to spray your fabric heavily with starch before cutting. Then, when handling the cut pieces, be very careful not to stretch the bias when pressing. Also, be sure to cut the largest pieces first to make the most of the yardage.

Center Star Block

9" finished

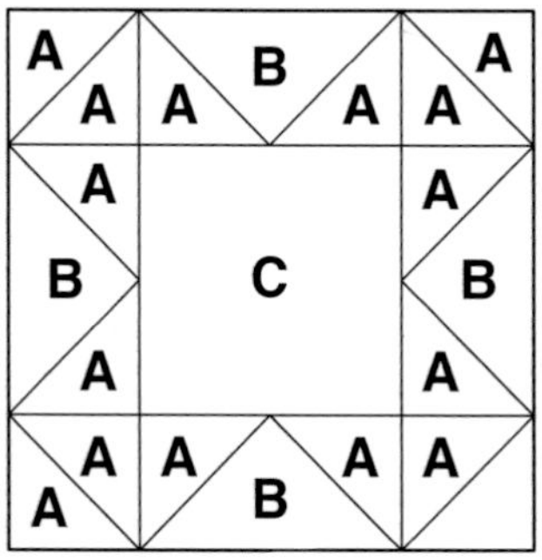

From medium tan print, cut:

❋ 2 – 3⅛" squares. Cut each in half on the diagonal to form 4 triangles (A).
❋ 1 – 5¾" square. Cut in half twice on each diagonal to form 4 triangles (B).

From black print #1, cut:

❋ 1 – 5" square (C).

From brown stripe, cut:

❋ 4 – 3⅛" squares. Cut each in half on the diagonal to form 8 triangles (A).

Fabrics

I yards of medium tan print
2 ½ yards black print #1 for quilt center and outer border
¾ yard brown stripe quilt center and inner border
¾ yards blue print
¼ yard blue dot print
⅜ yard blue stripe
¼ yard brown plaid
⅝ yard navy print
1 ¼ yard black print #2
2 yard light tan print
⅞ yard black print #3 for binding
8 ⅜ yards for backing

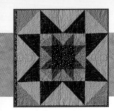

From blue print, cut:

✳ 2 – 3⅛" squares. Cut each in half on the diagonal to form 4 triangles (A).

Piecing for Center Star

✳ Make 4 rectangle units. Sew 2 brown stripe triangles (A) to each short edges of the medium tan print triangles (B) to make a rectangle. Press to the brown.

Make 4

✳ Make 4 half-square triangle units. Sew 4 blue print triangles (A) to 4 medium tan print triangles (A) to make half-square triangle units. Press to the blue.

Make 4

✳ Sew two of the rectangles to opposite sides of the black print #1 square (C).

✳ Sew 1 half-square triangle unit to opposite ends of the remaining two rectangles.

Make 2

✳ Referring to the block diagram, sew these units together to form the Center Star.

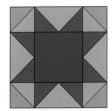

Round 2:

From light tan print background, cut:

✳ 2 – 5⅜" squares. Cut each in half on the diagonal to form 4 triangles (D).

✳ 1 – 10¼" square. Cut in half twice on each diagonal to form 4 triangles (E).

From brown plaid, cut:

✳ 4 – 5⅜" squares. Cut each in half on the diagonal to form 8 triangles (D).

From blue dot print cut:

✳ 2 – 5⅜" squares. Cut each in half on the diagonal to form 4 triangles (D).

✳ Assemble half-square triangle units and rectangle units as instructed in the Center Star block above. Sew 2 rectangle units to either side of the Center Star block, referring to the diagram for placement. Press to the rectangle units. Sew 2 half-square triangle units to either side of 1 rectangle unit. Press to the rectangle unit.

✳ Repeat with remaining rectangle and half-square triangle units. Sew to the top and bottom of the Center Star block. Press to the outside.

✳ Reminder: Take care not to stretch the bias on triangle (E) as you are sewing and pressing.

Round 3:

From medium tan print, cut:
✳ 2 – 9⅞" squares. Cut each in half on the diagonal to form 4 triangles (F).
✳ 1 – 19¼" square. Cut in half twice on each diagonal to form 4 triangles (G).

From navy print, cut:
✳ 4 – 9⅞" squares. Cut each in half on the diagonal to form 8 triangles (F).

From blue stripe, cut:
✳ 2 – 9⅞" squares. Cut each in half on the diagonal to form 4 triangles (F).

✳ Assemble half-square triangle units and rectangle units as instructed in the Center Star block above. Sew 2 rectangle units to either side of Round 2, referring to the diagram for placement. Press to the rectangle units. Sew 2 half-square triangle units to either side of 1 rectangle unit. Press to the rectangle unit.

✳ Repeat with remaining rectangle and half-square triangle units. Sew to the top and bottom of Round 2. Press to the outside.

✳ Reminder: Take care not to stretch the bias on triangle (G) as you are sewing and pressing.

Round 4

From light tan print cut:
✳ 2 – 18⅞" squares. Cut each in half on the diagonal to form 4 triangles (H).
✳ 1 – 37¼" square. Cut in half twice on each diagonal to form 4 triangles (I).

From black print #2 cut:
✳ 4 – 18⅞" x 18⅞" squares. Cut each in half on the diagonal to form 8 triangles (H).

From blue print cut:
✳ 2 – 18⅞" x 18⅞" squares. Cut each in half on the diagonal to form 4 triangles (H).

✳ Assemble half-square triangle units and rectangle units as instructed in the Center Star block above. Sew 2 rectangle units to either side of Round 3, referring to the diagram for placement. Press to the rectangle units. Sew 2 half-square triangle units to either side of 1 rectangle unit. Press to the rectangle unit.

✳ Repeat with remaining rectangle and half-square triangle units. Sew to the top and bottom of Round 3. Press to the outside.

✳ Reminder: Take care not to stretch the bias on triangle (I) as you are sewing and pressing.

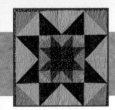
Borders
Inner border
From Brown stripe, cut:

✻ 8 – 2" strips x the width of fabric.

✻ Measure your quilt top from top to bottom through the center. Piece together inner border strips to make two strips equal to this measurement. Sew the strips on each side of the quilt.

✻ Measure your quilt top again from side to side through the center. Piece together inner border strips to make two strips equal to this measurement. Sew the strips to the top and bottom of the quilt.

Outer border
The outer border is made from black print strips with 4 pieced Center Star blocks for cornerstones.

From the black print #1, cut:

✻ 4 – 10½" strips x the length of fabric.

✻ Measure your quilt top through the center to find the length to piece the border strips. Add ½" to this measurement and trim the four border strips to this length. Set aside.

✻ Make 4 – 10" finished Center Star blocks for the four corners of the quilt. Refer to the instructions above to make the Center Star blocks, and use these cutting instructions.

To make one block
From medium tan background, cut:

✻ 2 – 3⅜" squares. Cut each in half on the diagonal to form 4 triangles (A).
✻ 1 – 6¼" square. Cut in half twice on each diagonal to form 4 triangles (B).

From black print #1, cut:

✻ 1 – 5½" square (C).

From brown print, cut:

✻ 4 – 3⅜" squares. Cut each in half on the diagonal to form 8 triangles (A).

From blue print, cut:

✻ 2 – 3⅜" squares. Cut each in half on the diagonal to form 4 triangles (A).

✻ Once the 4 cornerstone blocks are made, sew each to the end of two of the border strips.

✻ Sew the two plain border strips to either side of the quilt. Then, sew the two border strips with the corner blocks to the top and bottom of the quilt. Press to the borders.

Finishing
Quilt as desired.

✻ From the binding fabric, cut 10 – 2½" wide strips. Piece strips together to make a continuous binding strip.

70" X 82"

Civil War Shoo Fly

MADE BY DOLORES SMITH AND DAWN GREGORY • QUILTED BY CONNIE GRESHAM

Dolores and Sarah have always loved the classic block patterns, Shoo Fly and Churn Dash. Finding creative ways to color and set together these simple blocks is always a fun way to experiment with fabric. In this quilt, Sarah designed a setting that placed light prints in the alternate blocks along with shoo fly blocks with dark backgrounds. Dolores then went to work finding a variety of 1800s prints and backgrounds in a whole range of colors which created a quilt that really sparkles. This design is a great way to dive into your stash and use up lots of different fabrics. A dark border print helps tie it all together.

Fabrics

3 ¼ yards of assorted medium and dark value assorted prints
4 ½ yards of assorted cream and tan prints
½ yard of dark tan print for the inner border
1 ¼ yards of blue gray print for the outer border
¾ yard of blue gray print for binding
5 yards backing

Note: For a more scrappy look, collect fat eighths of the medium/dark and cream/tan prints.

To Make the Quilt

Civil War Shoo Fly includes 60 – 6" finished blocks.

From the assorted medium and dark prints, cut:

* 120 – 2⅞" squares cutting once on the diagonal to make 240 triangles (B).
* 240 – 2½" squares (A).
* Note: Each Shoo Fly block is made of one medium/dark print. Cut a minimum of 2 – 2⅞" squares and 4 – 2½" squares from each fabric.

From the assorted cream and tan prints, cut:

* 120 – 2⅞" squares cutting once on the diagonal to make 240 triangles (B).
* 60 – 2½" squares for block centers (A).
* 60 - 6½" squares for setting squares.
* Note: Each Shoo Fly block is made of one cream/tan print. Cut a minimum of 2 – 2⅞" squares and 1 – 2½" square from each fabric.
* Note: Reserve the leftover fabric for the border blocks.

Half-square triangle units

* Make 240.
* Stitch each medium/dark triangle (B) to each cream/tan triangle (B). Press to the dark.

Piecing for 1 Shoo Fly block

✳ Lay out 4 matching half-square triangle units, 4 matching medium/dark squares and 1 cream/tan square into 3 rows of 3 units each, as shown in the piecing diagram.

Make 60

✳ Stitch the rows together pressings seams toward the dark squares (A). Join rows together pressing seams in one direction.

✳ Make 60 blocks.

Quilt top assembly

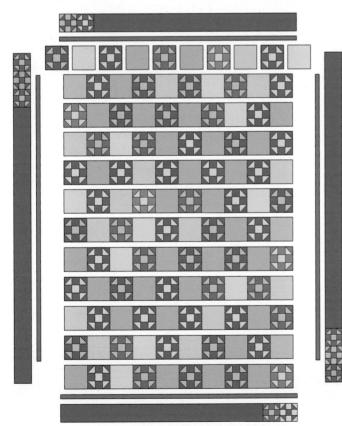

✳ Lay out 120 blocks alternating a Shoo Fly block with a setting block as shown in the assembly diagram. Sew the quilt together in 12 rows of 10 blocks each

Borders

Inner border

From the inner border print, cut:

✳ 8 strips – 1½" wide strips x the width of the fabric.

✳ Measure your quilt top from top to bottom through the center. Piece together inner border strips to make two strips equal to this measurement. Sew the strips on each side of the quilt.

✳ Measure your quilt top again from side to side through the center. Piece together inner border strips to make two strips equal to this measurement. Sew the strips to the top and bottom of the quilt.

Outer border

✳ The outer border is made of 10 – 4½" finished Shoo Fly blocks, six with a cream/tan center square and medium/ dark background squares and four with a medium/dark center square and cream/tan background squares, plus 4½" wide finished border strips.

Shoo Fly border blocks

From the assorted medium and dark prints, cut:
✳ 20 – 2⅜" squares cutting once on the diagonal to make 40 triangles (B).
✳ 28 – 2" squares (A).

From the assorted cream and tan prints, cut:
✳ 20 – 2⅜" squares cutting once on the diagonal to make 40 triangles (B).
✳ 22 – 2" square (A).

✳ Make 10 Shoo Fly blocks, follow the piecing instructions above. Referring to the block diagrams below, make 6 with a cream/tan center square (A) and 4 with medium/dark center square (A).

Make 6

Make 4

From the top and bottom outer border print, cut:
✳ 3 strips – 5" wide strips x the width of fabric. Sew together into one long strip.

✳ Measure your quilt top from side to side through the center. Note that measurement. Referring to the quilt assembly diagram, sew 1 medium/dark center block to 1 cream/tan center block. Sew the border strip to the cream/tan center block. Cut the border to your measurement and sew to the top of the quilt top. Repeat to make the bottom border using 1 medium/dark center block, 1 cream/tan center block and the remaining top and bottom border strip.

To make the side border strips, cut:
✳ 4– 5" wide strips x the width of fabric. Sew together into one long strip.

✳ Measure your quilt top from top to bottom through the center. Note that measurement. Referring to the quilt assembly diagram, sew 1 medium/dark center block in between 2 cream/tan center blocks. Sew the border strip to 1 of the cream/tan center blocks. Cut the border to your measurement. Refer to the diagram and sew to one side of the quilt top so the Shoo Fly blocks are one the same corner as the top border. Repeat to make the other side border using 1 medium/dark center block, two cream/tan center blocks and the remaining side border strip.

Finishing
Quilt as desired.

From the binding fabric, cut:
✳ 8 – 2½" wide strips.
✳ Piece strips together to make a continuous binding strip. Bind.

50" X 41"

Apple Blossom Buds

DESIGNED BY DOLORES SMITH • STITCHED BY GLADYS SCHNEIDER • QUILTED BY CONNIE GRESHAM

Let this table runner, Apple Blossom Buds, add a warm, festive feel to your family gatherings. Dolores saw another opportunity to take the Love Apple pattern and work with wonderful hand-dyed wools and 1800s browns. Brown is one of Dolores's favorite colors (with red being a close second) so the outer border print which combines these two colors was a perfect choice to finish the project.

Cutting

From the background muslin, cut:

❋ 1 – width of fabric x 45" rectangle. Press the background in half vertically, then again horizontally to find the center of the background fabric.

Appliqué

Referring to the fusible webbing package, prepare all the appliqué shapes. Templates are on pages 104-107.

❋ For the bias stems, cut the 20" x 20" square on the diagonal corner to corner once. Cutting along the diagonal edge, cut 7 bias strips ¾" wide. Strips cut on the bias will allow you to curve them easily.

Fabrics

Cotton:
1¼ yards aged muslin for background
⅔ yard brown for inner border and binding
⅔ yard brown print for outer border
3 yards brown for backing

Wool:

3" x 6" gold (D)
6" x 20" dark red (B) (E & Er)
5½" x 22" dark green (F & Fr)
5" x 12" medium red (A)
8" x 20" light red (C)
6" x 20" red for berries (G)
2" x 10" tan for trim on vase
14" square brown for vase
20" square medium green for stems

Additional Supplies

Perle cotton size #8 in colors to match the wool
Chenille Needle
Fusible webbing

* Following the assembly diagram, layout all the appliqué pieces and stems except for the vase. Pin the stems in place. Trim the ends of the flowers and stems, leaving about 1" of each stem under where the vase will be placed. Lay the vase piece in place and press all the pieces down.

* Stitch around each shape using a primitive whip stitch. When all the pieces are stitched down trim up the background to 33½" x 42½".

Borders

Inner border
From the inner border fabric, cut:
* 5 – 1½" wide strips x the width of the fabric.

* Measure your quilt top from top to bottom through the center. Piece together inner border strips to make two strips equal to this measurement. Sew the strips on each side of the quilt.

* Measure your quilt top again from side to side through the center. Piece together inner border strips to make two strips equal to this measurement. Sew the strips to the top and bottom of the quilt.

Outer border
From the outer border fabric, cut:
* 5 – 3½" strips x the width of the fabric.

* Measure your quilt top from top to bottom through the center. Piece together outer border strips to make two strips equal to this measurement. Sew the strips on each side of the quilt.

* Measure your quilt top again from side to side through the center. Piece together outer border strips to make two strips equal to this measurement. Sew the strips to the top and bottom of the quilt.

Finishing
Quilt as desired.

From the binding fabric, cut:
* 5 – 2¼" strips x the width of fabric.
* Piece strips together to make a continuous binding strip. Bind.

47" X 16½"

Twilight Serenity

MADE BY DOLORES SMITH

Using the Oak Leaves and Flowers pattern, Dolores decided to enlarge the medallion to give a classic look for a warm bed pillow. She loves the feel and look of dark, rich hand-dyed wool, so she tries to use wool in her quilting whenever possible.

The pillow is a perfect companion to the Starry Nights quilt. To tie the two together, Dolores selected several cotton prints to use as a prairie point edging on the pillow. When you're ready to change the look of a room or to update a piece of furniture, consider making these large-size pillows. Pillows are an inexpensive and quick way to change the look of a room.

To Make the Pillow
From the wool plaid background, cut:
❋ I – 18" x 60" rectangle. Press the background in half vertically, then again horizontally to find the center of the background fabric.

Appliqué
Referring to the fusible webbing package, prepare all the appliqué shapes. Templates are found on pages 108-109.

Following the assembly diagram, lay the center medallion piece on the background fabric. Then add the other appliqué shapes. Press in place. Use matching thread color for each shape, machine stitch around the appliqué shapes using a buttonhole stitch. Trim the pillow top to 17" x 48½".

Fabrics
Cotton:
⅛ yard stripe for inner trim
¼ yard of 7 different prints
    for prairie points
I yard for backing

Wool:
½ yard tan plaid for background
4" x 10" red for appliqué (A and D)
4" x 5" light tan for appliqué (B)
5" x 5" gold for appliqué (C and E)
5" x 5" blue for appliqué (F)
½ yard black for medallion (G)

Additional supplies:
Fusible webbing
50 wt. thread in colors to match
    the appliqué pieces
Polyfil stuffing

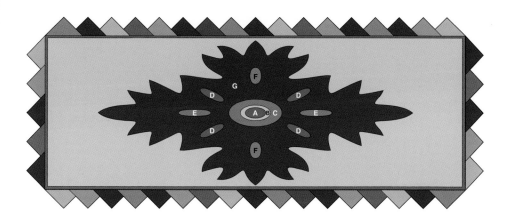

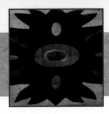
Finishing

To make the trim, cut:

❋ 5 – 1" wide strips of striped fabric x the width of fabric. Join together to make 1 strip long enough to go around the pillow top. Press the strip in half widthwise, wrong side's together to make the trim. Then pin the trim to the outside raw edge of the pillow top and baste in place.

Prairie Points

From the 7 assorted prints, cut:

❋ 44 – 5" squares.
❋ Fold each square, wrong sides together, on the diagonal to form a triangle and press. Fold in half again to make another triangle and press.

❋ Place one triangle at the top left corner of your pillow, with raw edges together and the opening of the triangle facing the right. Open this triangle and place another triangle inside the first one so it is about half way in the first triangle. Continue on in this manner until you have encircled the entire pillow top. Baste the triangles in place by hand or by using the longest stitch on your machine.

Finishing

Piece the backing to 17" x 48½". Place the top and backing, right sides together and sew with a ⅝" seam allowance leaving a opening for stuffing. Turn right side out and stuff with polyfil. Hand stitch the opening shut.

Missouri Puzzle templates

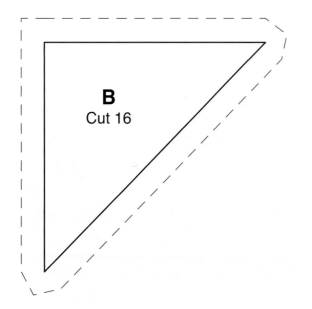

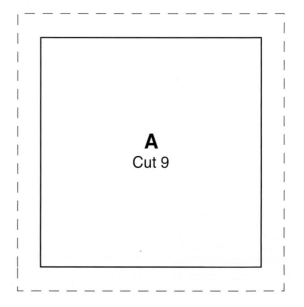

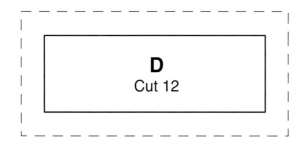

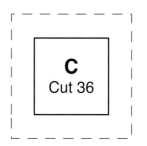

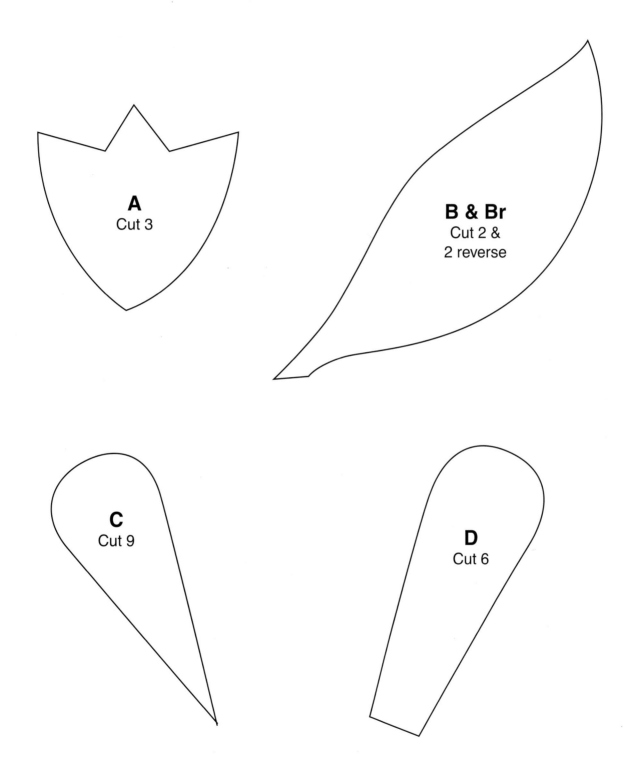

A
Cut 3

B & Br
Cut 2 &
2 reverse

C
Cut 9

D
Cut 6

Framed Variable Star templates

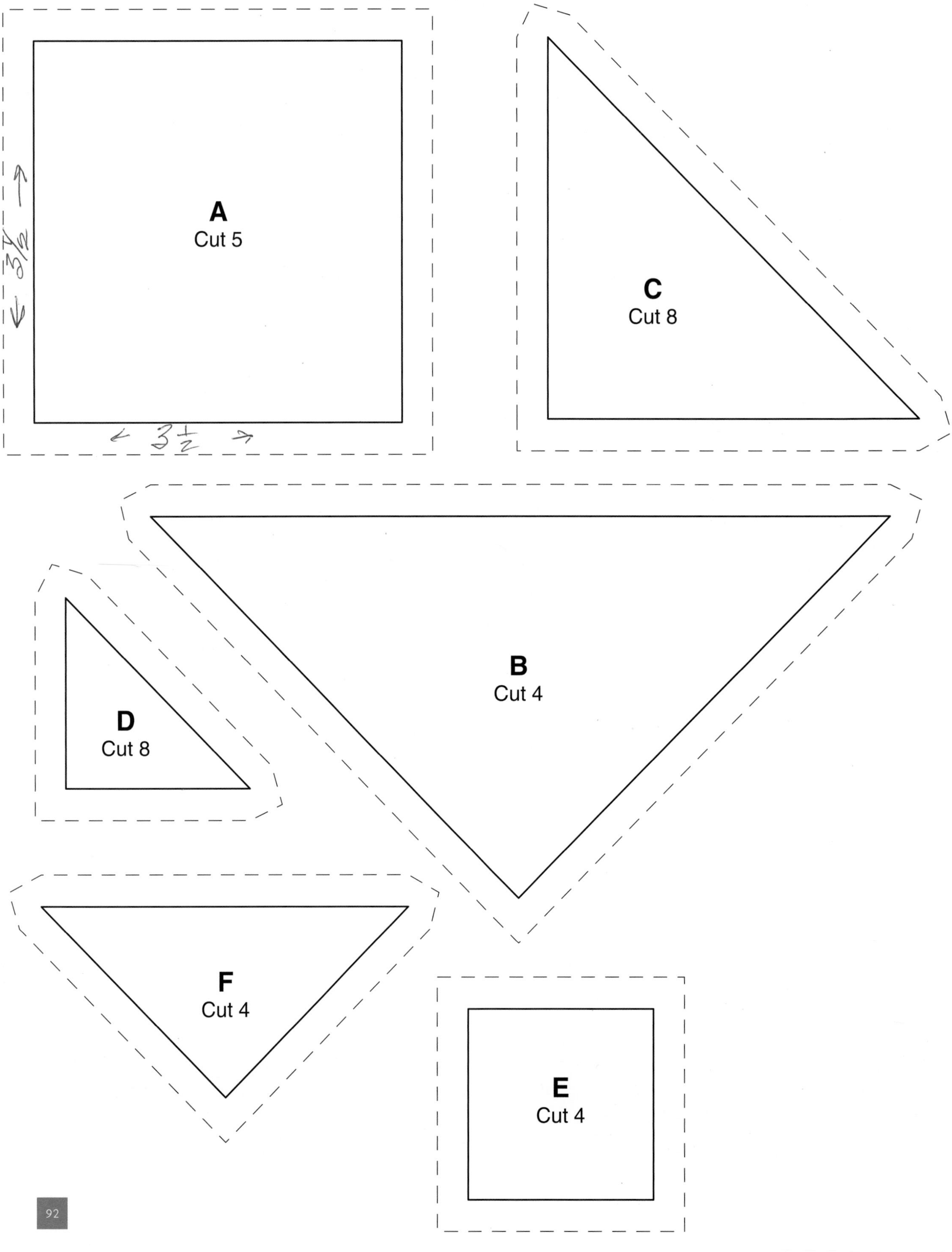

A
Cut 5

$3\frac{1}{2}$

$3\frac{1}{2}$

C
Cut 8

B
Cut 4

D
Cut 8

F
Cut 4

E
Cut 4

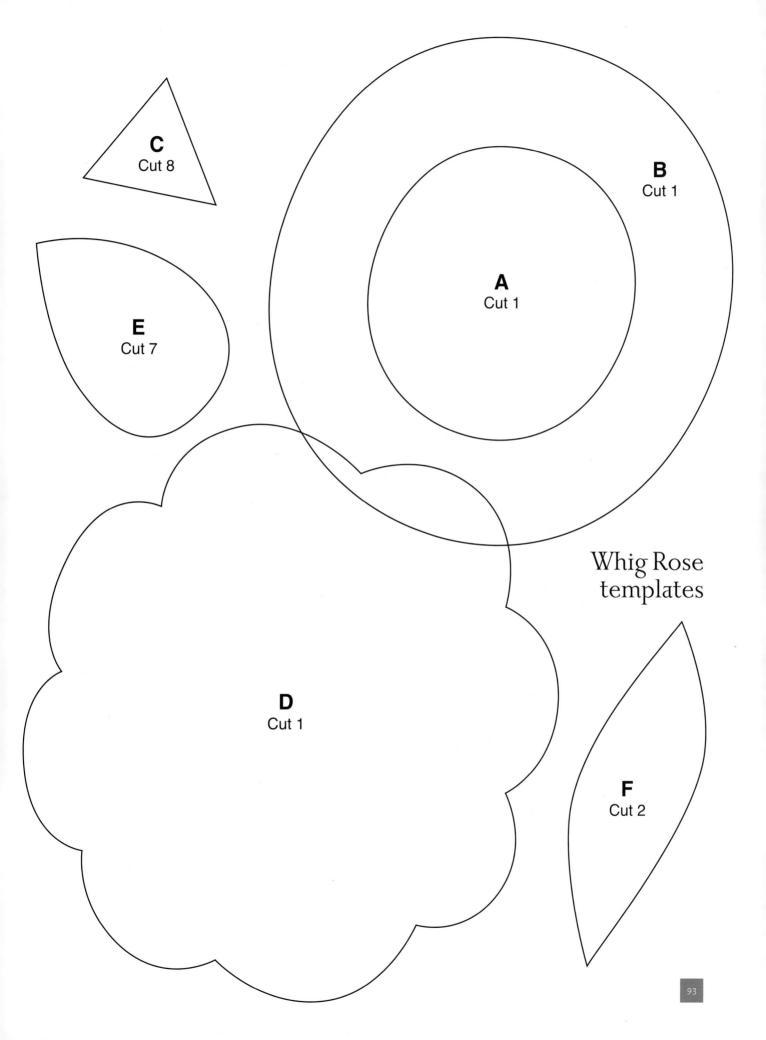

C
Cut 8

B
Cut 1

A
Cut 1

E
Cut 7

Whig Rose
templates

D
Cut 1

F
Cut 2

Four X templates

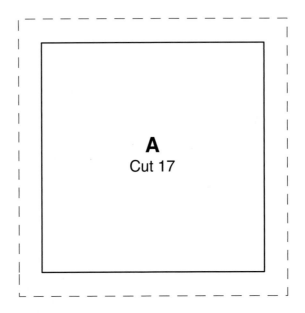

A
Cut 17

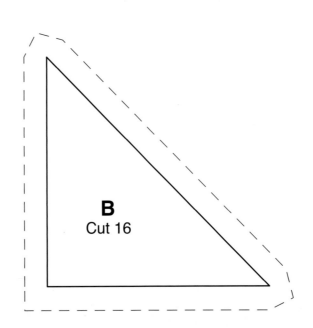

B
Cut 16

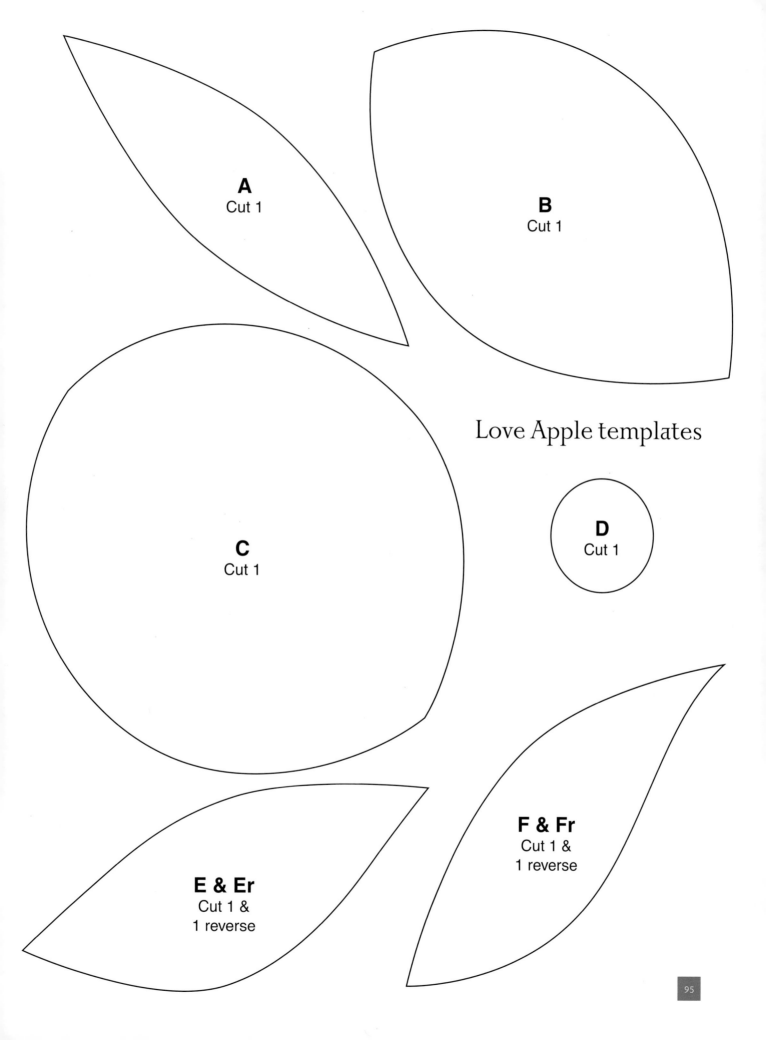

A
Cut 1

B
Cut 1

Love Apple templates

C
Cut 1

D
Cut 1

E & Er
Cut 1 &
1 reverse

F & Fr
Cut 1 &
1 reverse

Tulip templates

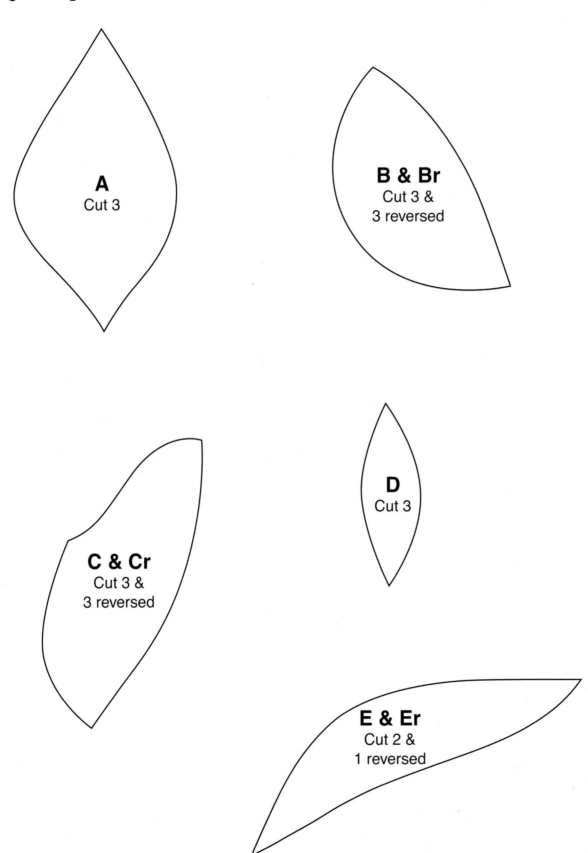

A
Cut 3

B & Br
Cut 3 &
3 reversed

C & Cr
Cut 3 &
3 reversed

D
Cut 3

E & Er
Cut 2 &
1 reversed

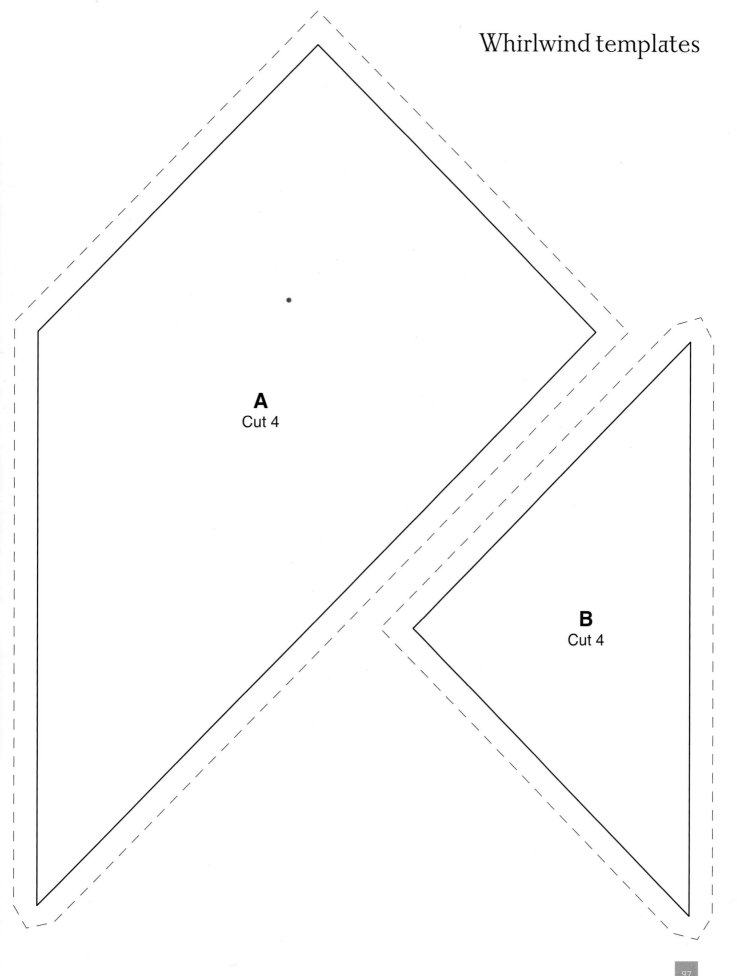

A
Cut 4

B
Cut 4

King's Crown templates

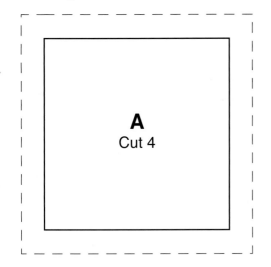

A
Cut 4

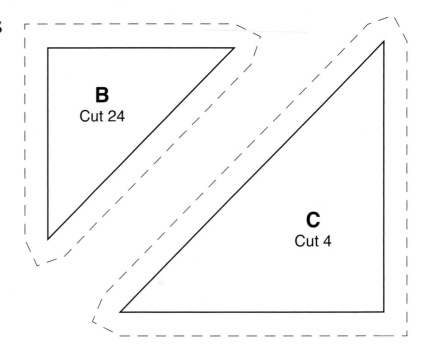

B
Cut 24

C
Cut 4

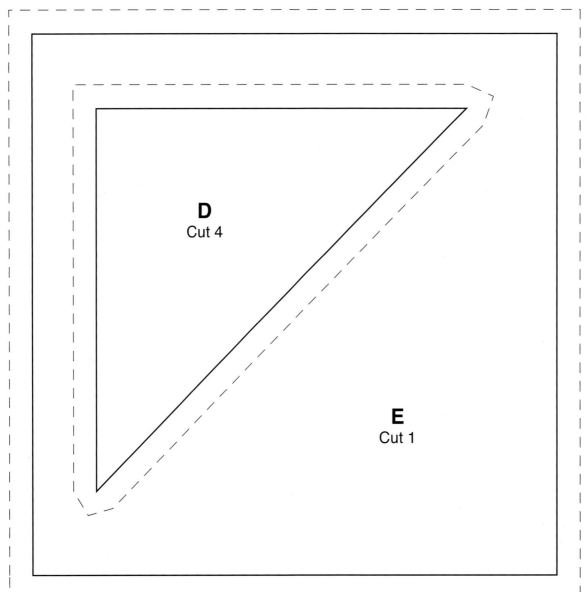

D
Cut 4

E
Cut 1

E
Cut 1

G
Cut 1

F
Cut 1

B
Cut 4

C
Cut 4

D
Cut 8

A
Cut 1

Place on fold

Place on fold

New York Beauty templates

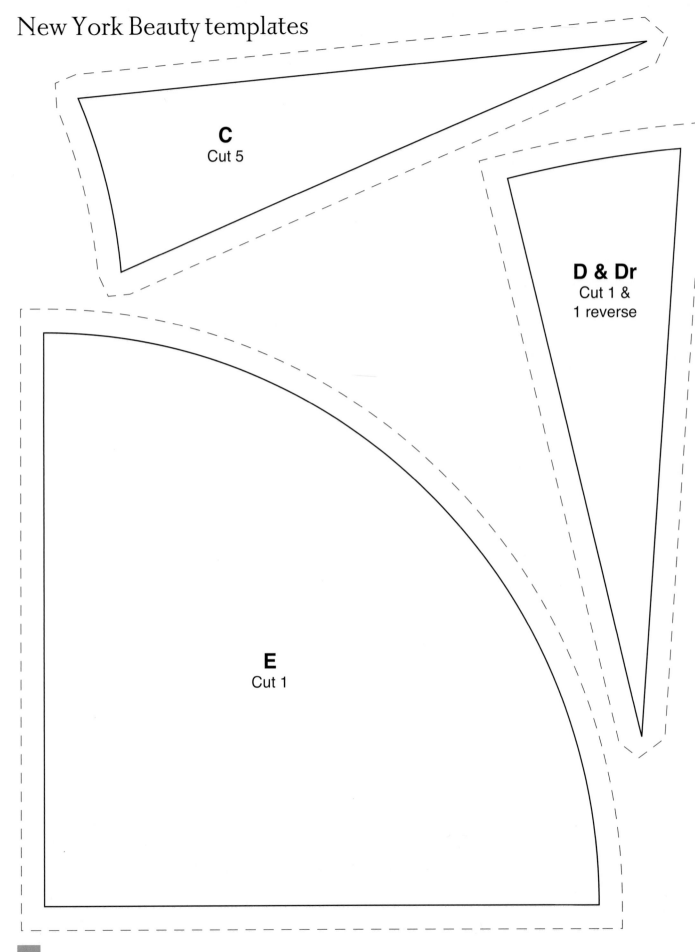

C
Cut 5

D & Dr
Cut 1 &
1 reverse

E
Cut 1

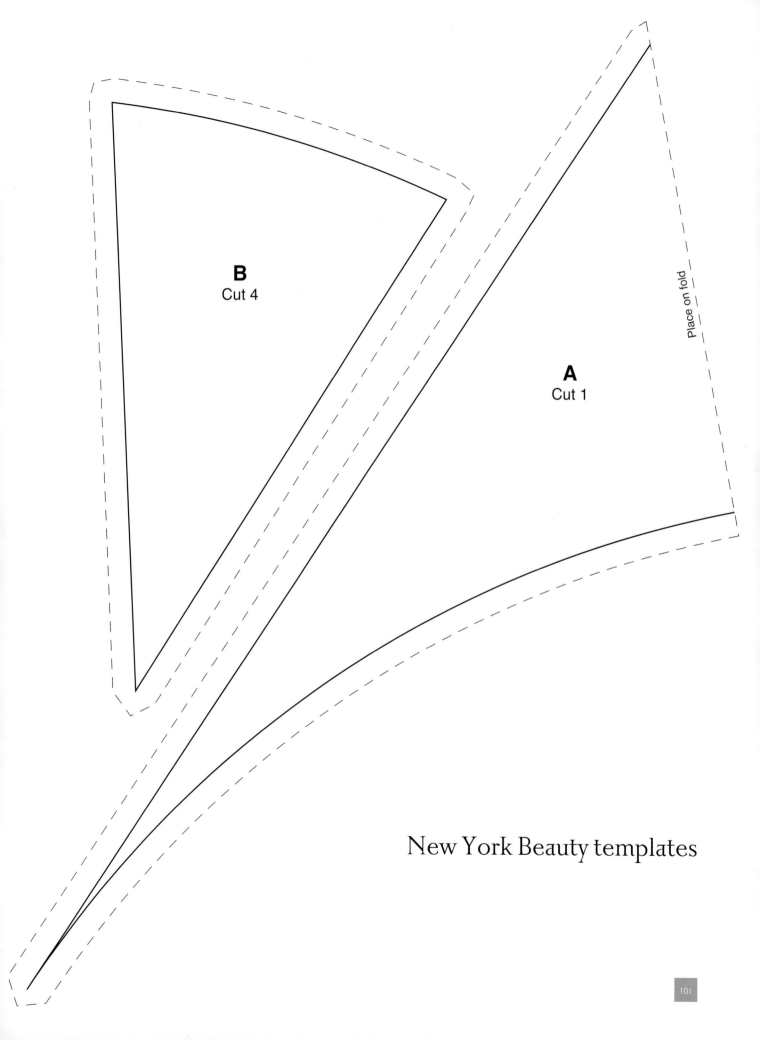

B
Cut 4

A
Cut 1

Place on fold

New York Beauty templates

New York Beauty paper piecing templates

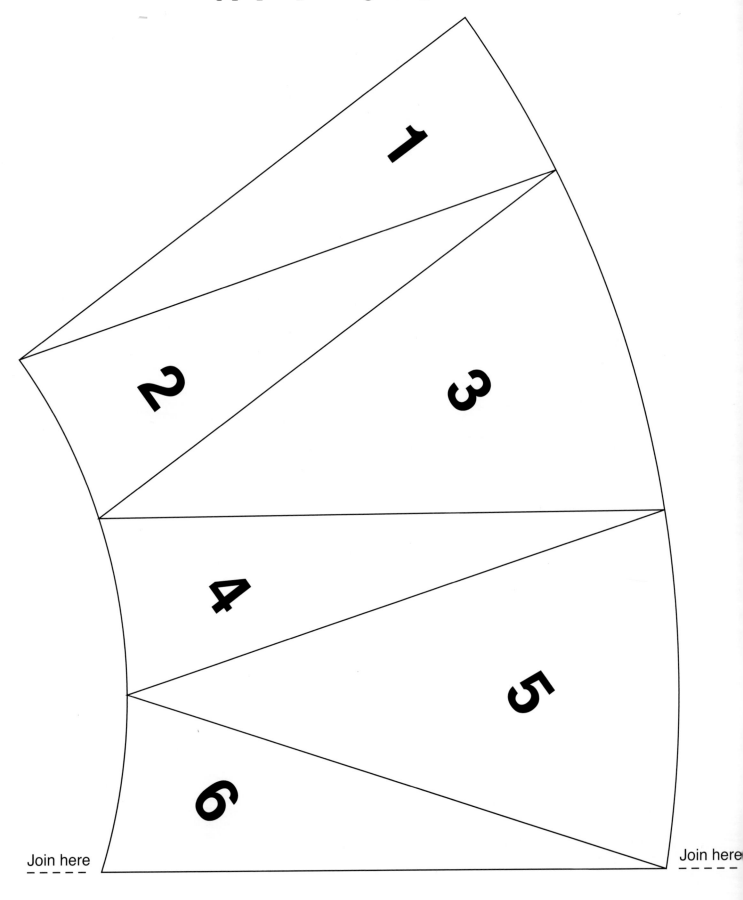

Join here

Join here

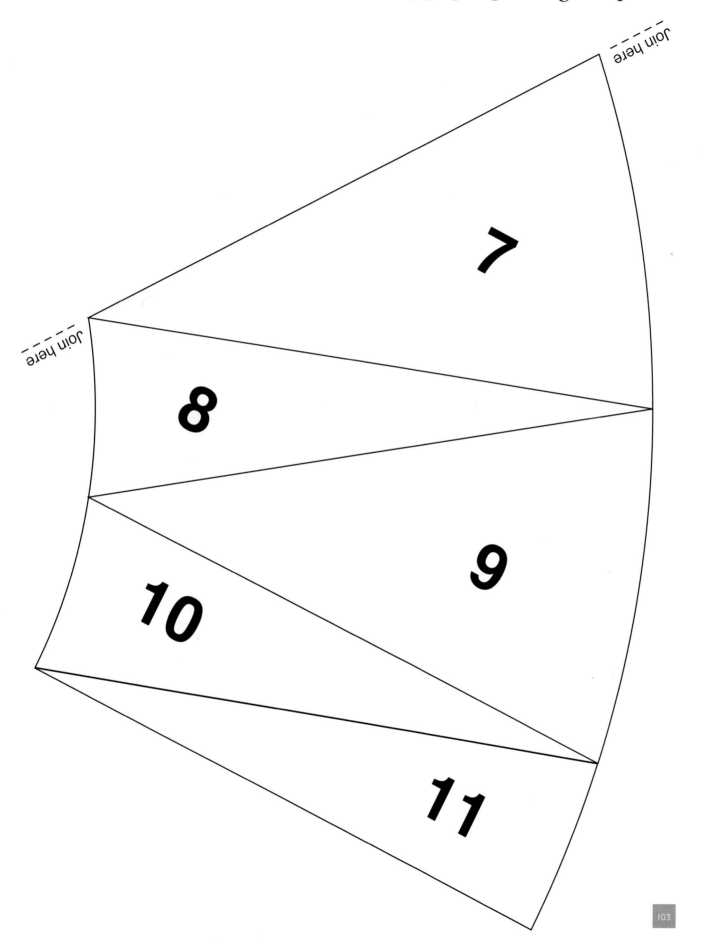

Join here

Join here

7

8

9

10

11

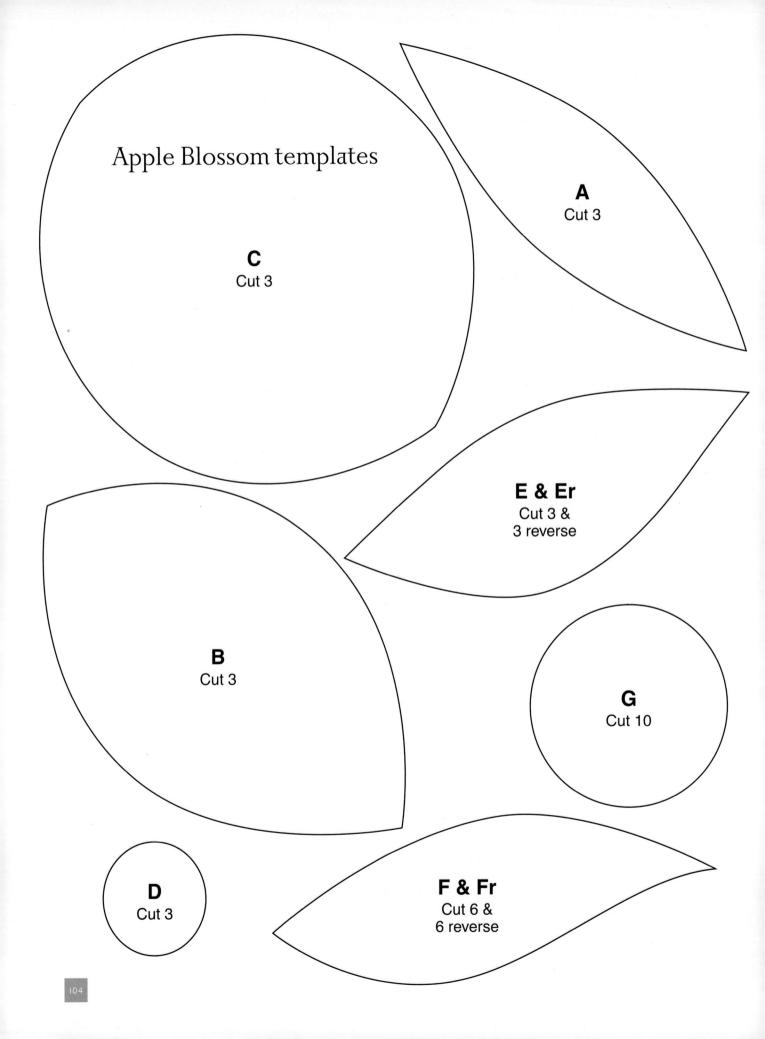

Apple Blossom templates

C
Cut 3

A
Cut 3

E & Er
Cut 3 &
3 reverse

B
Cut 3

G
Cut 10

D
Cut 3

F & Fr
Cut 6 &
6 reverse

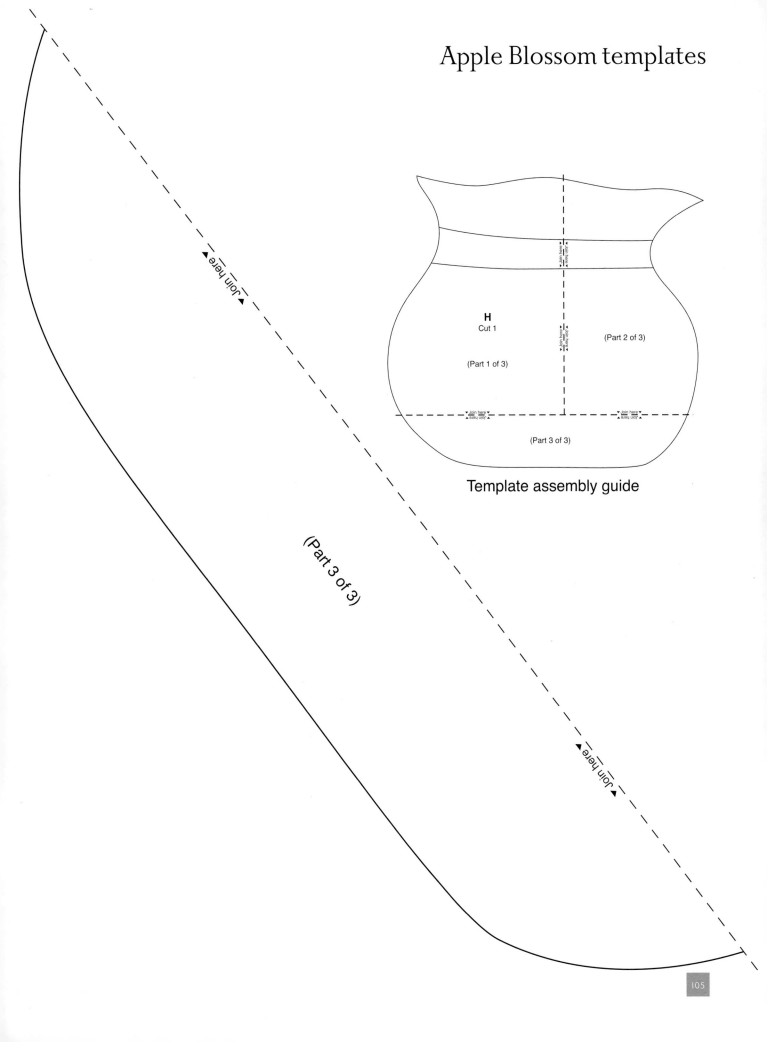

Template assembly guide

H
Cut 1

(Part 1 of 3)

(Part 2 of 3)

(Part 3 of 3)

(Part 3 of 3)

Join here

Join here

Apple Blossom templates

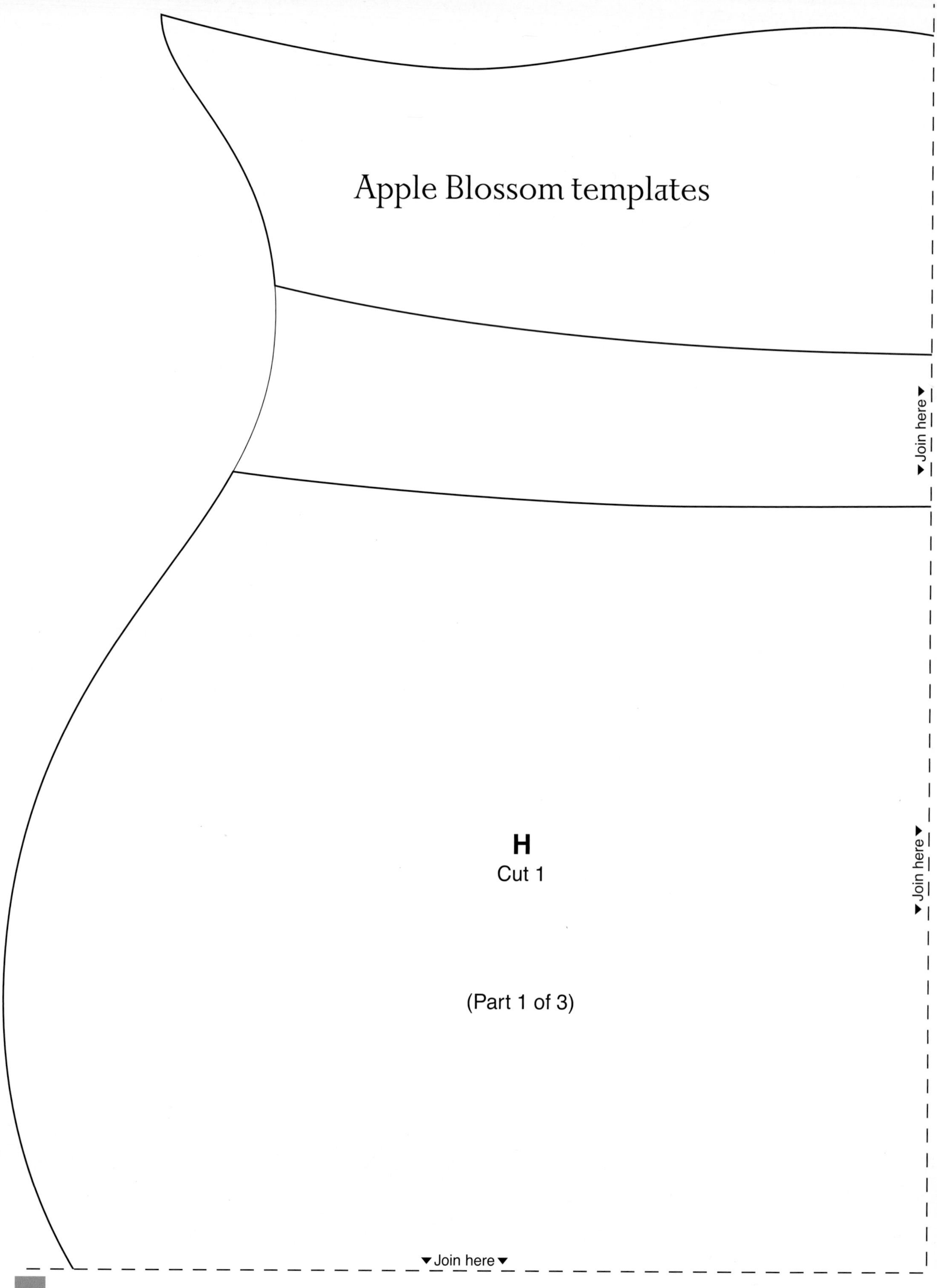

H

Cut 1

(Part 1 of 3)

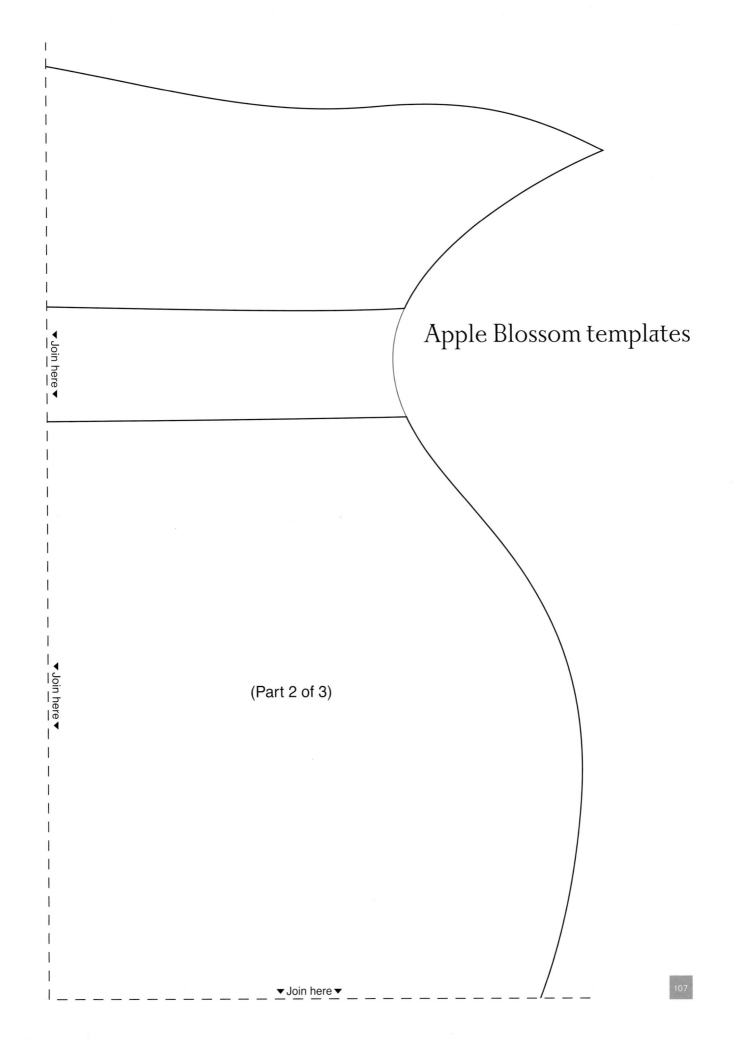

Apple Blossom templates

(Part 2 of 3)

Twighlight Serenity templates

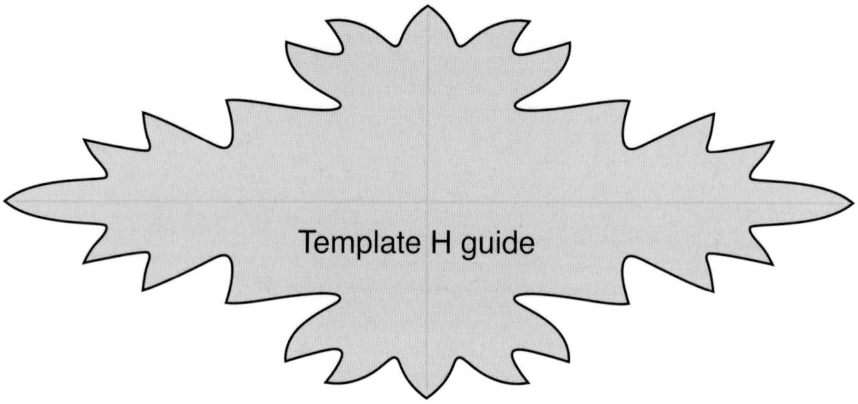

Template H guide

H
Cut 1

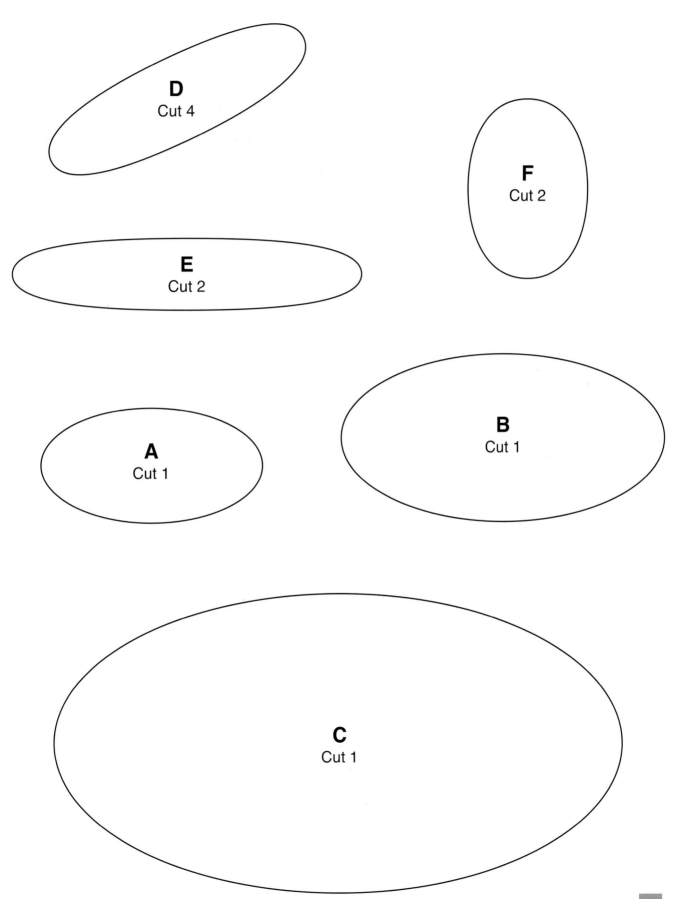

Framing Star and Inner Border templates

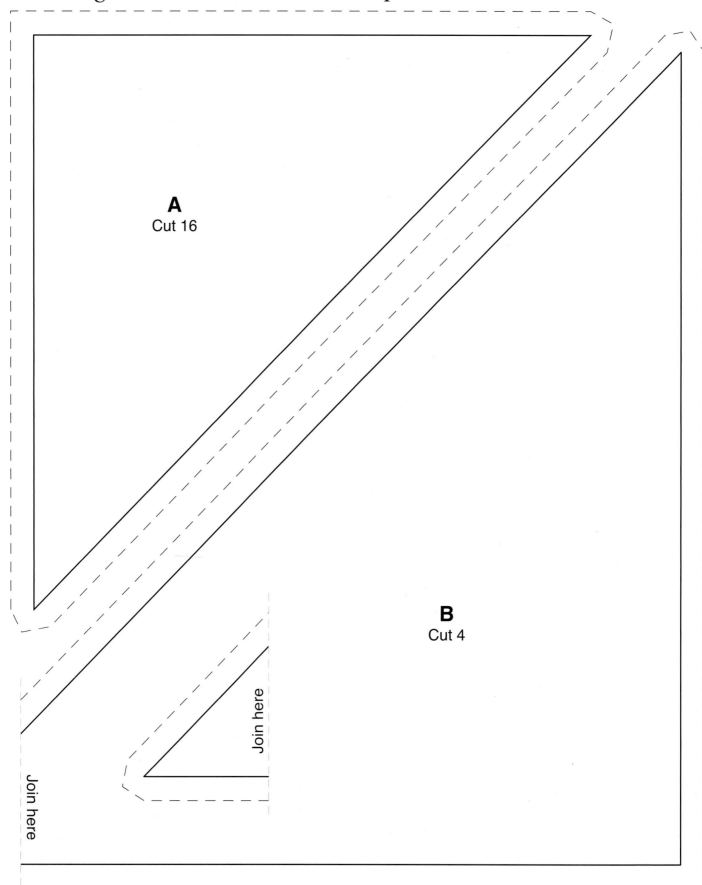

A

Cut 16

B

Cut 4

Join here

Join here

Join here

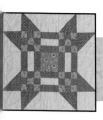

Bibliography

Baker, Susan M. "Biographical History of Pottawattmie Co., IA - Amelia BLOOMER."
    RootsWeb Genealogical Data Cooperative. Web. 10 Aug. 2009.
    http://homepages.rootsweb.ancestry.com/~gonfishn/bhopci/b/bloomera.html.

"Carrie Chapman Catt biography." *Protect Library Funding*. Web. 30 June 2009.
    http://www.lkwdpl.org/wihohio/catt-car.htm.

"Coppin, Fannie Jackson (1837-1913) | The Black Past: Remembered and Reclaimed."
    | The Black Past: Remembered and Reclaimed. Web. 30 June 2009.
    http://www.blackpast.org/?q=aah/coppin-fannie-jackson-1837-1913.

"Elizabeth Cady Stanton." *Spartacus Educational — Home Page*. Web. 30 June 2009.
    http://www.spartacus.schoolnet.co.uk/USAWstanton.htm.

"Frances Perkins (1880 - 1965)." *Www.aflcio.org — America's Union Movement* . Web. 30
    June 2009. http://www.aflcio.org/aboutus/history/history/perkins.cfm.

"Jane Addams - Biography." *Nobelprize.org*. Web. 30 June 2009.
    http://nobelprize.org/nobel_prizes/peace/laureates/1931/addams-bio.html.

"Julia Ward Howe Biography." *Julia Ward Howe - Home*. Web. 30 June 2009.
    http://www.juliawardhowe.org/bio.htm.

"Lucretia Mott." *Women's History - Comprehensive Women's History Research Guide*. Web. 30 June
    2009.
    http://www.womenshistory.about.com/od/suffragepre1848/p/lucretia_mott.htm.

"Lucy Stone — A Soul As Free As the Air." *Women's History - Comprehensive Women's History
    Research Guide*. Web. 30 June 2009.
    http://womenshistory.about.com/od/stonelucy/a/lucy_stone.htm.

"Mary Church Terrell." *Tennessee State University: Welcome to Your Future!* Web. 30 June 2009.
    http://www.tnstate.edu/library/digital/terrell.htm.

"Sojourner Truth biography." *Protect Library Funding*. Web. 30 June 2009.
    http://www.lkwdpl.org/wihohio/trut-soj.htm.

"Susan B. Anthony Biography." *The Official Susan B. Anthony House*. Web. 30 June 2009.
    http://www.susanbanthonyhouse.org/biography.shtml.

Other Star Quilts Books

New for 2009

❋ *Flora Botanica: Quilts from the Spencer Museum of Art* by Barbara Brackman

❋ *Making Memories: Simple Quilts from Cherished Clothing* by Deb Rowden

❋ *Pots de Fleurs: A Garden of Applique Techniques* by Kathy Delaney

❋ *Wedding Ring, Pickle Dish and More: Paper Piecing Curves* by Carolyn McCormick

❋ *The Graceful Garden: A Jacobean Fantasy Quilt* by Denise Sheehan

❋ *My Stars: Patterns from The Kansas City Star, Volume I*

❋ *Opening Day: 14 Quilts Celebrating the Life and Times of Negro Leagues Baseball* by Sonie Ruffin

❋ *St. Louis Stars: Nine Unique Quilts that Spark* by Toby Lischko

❋ *Whimsyland: Be Cre8ive with Lizzie B* by Liz & Beth Hawkins

❋ *Cradle to Cradle* by Barbara Jones of Quilt Soup

❋ *Pick of the Seasons: Quilts to Inspire You Through the Year* by Tammy Johnson and Avis Shirer of Joined at the Hip

❋ *Across the Pond: Projects Inspired by Quilts of the British Isles* by Bettina Havig

❋ *Flags of the American Revolution* by Jan Patek

❋ *Get Your Stitch on Route 66: Quilts from the Mother Road* by Christina DeArmond, Eula Lang and Kaye Spitzli from Of One Mind

❋ *Gone to Texas: Quilts from a Pioneer Woman's Journals* by Betsy Chutchian

❋ *My Stars II: Patterns from The Kansas City Star, Volume II*

❋ *Nature's Offerings: Primitive Projects Inspired by the Four Seasons* by Maggie Bonanomi

❋ *Quilts of the Golden West: Mining the History of the Gold and Silver Rush* by Cindy Brick